SYLVIA PLATH (October 27, 1932 – February 11, 1963) was an American poet, novelist, and short-story writer. She is credited with advancing the genre of confessional poetry and is best known for two of her published collections, The Colossus and Other Poems (1960) and Ariel (1965), as well as The Bell Jar, a semi-autobiographical novel published shortly before her death in 1963. The Collected Poems were published in 1981, which included previously unpublished works. For this collection Plath was awarded a Pulitzer Prize in Poetry in 1982, making her the fourth to receive this honour posthumously.

Sylvia Plath

100 SELECTED POEMS

DELHI OPEN BOOKS

100 SELECTED POEMS
BY SYLVIA PLATH

Edition copyright © Delhi Open Books, 2022

Published by

Delhi Open Books

G/F, 4771/23, Bharat Ram Road, Daryaganj, New Delhi-110002
Ph.: 91-11-42408081
E-mail: delhiopenbooks2016@gmail.com

ISBN: 978-93-94109-58-2

Cover, Typesetting, and Book Design by ROHIT

Printed & bound in India

Contents

A Better Resurrection

I have no wit, I have no words, no tears;
My heart within me like a stone
Is numbed too much for hopes or fears;
Look right, look left, I dwell alone;
A lift mine eyes, but dimmed with grief
No everlasting hills I see;
My life is like the falling leaf;
O Jesus, quicken me.

A Birthday Present

What is this, behind this veil, is it ugly, is it beautiful?
It is shimmering, has it breasts, has it edges?
I am sure it is unique, I am sure it is what I want.
When I am quiet at my cooking I feel it looking, I feel it thinking
'Is this the one I am too appear for,
Is this the elect one, the one with black eye-pits and a scar?
Measuring the flour, cutting off the surplus,
Adhering to rules, to rules, to rules.
Is this the one for the annunciation?
My god, what a laugh!'
But it shimmers, it does not stop, and I think it wants me.
I would not mind if it were bones, or a pearl button.
I do not want much of a present, anyway, this year.
After all I am alive only by accident.
I would have killed myself gladly that time any possible way.
Now there are these veils, shimmering like curtains,
The diaphanous satins of a January window
White as babies' bedding and glittering with dead breath. O ivory!
It must be a tusk there, a ghost column.
Can you not see I do not mind what it is.
Can you not give it to me?
Do not be ashamed--I do not mind if it is small.
Do not be mean, I am ready for enormity.
Let us sit down to it, one on either side, admiring the gleam,
The glaze, the mirrory variety of it.
Let us eat our last supper at it, like a hospital plate.
I know why you will not give it to me,
You are terrified
The world will go up in a shriek, and your
head with it,
Bossed, brazen, an antique shield,
A marvel to your great-grandchildren.
Do not be afraid, it is not so.

A Lesson In Vengeance

In the dour ages
Of drafty cells and draftier castles,
Of dragons breathing without the frame of fables,
Saint and king unfisted obstruction's knuckles
By no miracle or majestic means,
But by such abuses
As smack of spite and the overscrupulous
Twisting of thumbscrews: one soul tied in sinews,
One white horse drowned, and all the unconquered pinnacles
Of God's city and Babylon's
Must wait, while here Suso's
Hand hones his tack and needles,
Scouraging to sores his own red sluices
For the relish of heaven, relentless, dousing with prickles
Of horsehair and lice his horny loins;
While there irate Cyrus
Squanders a summer and the brawn of his heroes
To rebuke the horse-swallowing River Gyndes:
He split it into three hundred and sixty trickles
A girl could wade without wetting her shins.
Still, latter-day sages,
Smiling at this behavior, subjugating their enemies
Neatly, nicely, by disbelief or bridges,
Never grip, as the grandsires did, that devil who chuckles
From grain of the marrow and the river-bed grains.
Submitted by Venus

A Life

Touch it: it won't shrink like an eyeball,
This egg-shaped bailiwick, clear as a tear.
Here's yesterday, last year ---
Palm-spear and lily distinct as flora in the vast
Windless threadwork of a tapestry.
Flick the glass with your fingernail:
It will ping like a Chinese chime in the slightest air stir
Though nobody in there looks up or bothers to answer.
The inhabitants are light as cork,
Every one of them permanently busy.
At their feet, the sea waves bow in single file.
Never trespassing in bad temper:
Stalling in midair,
Short-reined, pawing like paradeground horses.
Overhead, the clouds sit tasseled and fancy
As Victorian cushions. This family
Of valentine faces might please a collector:
They ring true, like good china.
Elsewhere the landscape is more frank.
The light falls without letup, blindingly.
A woman is dragging her shadow in a circle
About a bald hospital saucer.
It resembles the moon, or a sheet of blank paper
And appears to have suffered a sort of private blitzkrieg.
She lives quietly
With no attachments, like a foetus in a bottle,
The obsolete house, the sea, flattened to a picture
She has one too many dimensions to enter.
Grief and anger, exorcised,
Leave her alone now.
The future is a grey seagull
Tattling in its cat-voice of departure.
Age and terror, like nurses, attend her,

And a drowned man, complaining of the great cold,
Crawls up out of the sea.
Submitted by Venus

Aftermath

Compelled by calamity's magnet
They loiter and stare as if the house
Burnt-out were theirs, or as if they thought
Some scandal might any minute ooze
From a smoke-choked closet into light;
No deaths, no prodigious injuries
Glut these hunters after an old meat,
Blood-spoor of the austere tragedies.
Mother Medea in a green smock
Moves humbly as any housewife through
Her ruined apartments, taking stock
Of charred shoes, the sodden upholstery:
Cheated of the pyre and the rack,
The crowd sucks her last tear and turns away.

Among the Narcissi

Spry, wry, and gray as these March sticks,
Percy bows, in his blue peajacket, among the narcissi.
He is recuperating from something on the lung.
The narcissi, too, are bowing to some big thing :
It rattles their stars on the green hill where Percy
Nurses the hardship of his stitches, and walks and walks.
There is a dignity to this; there is a formality-
The flowers vivid as bandages, and the man mending.
They bow and stand : they suffer such attacks!
And the octogenarian loves the little flocks.
He is quite blue; the terrible wind tries his breathing.
The narcissi look up like children, quickly and whitely.

An Appearance

The smile of iceboxes annihilates me.
Such blue currents in the veins of my loved one!
I hear her great heart purr.
From her lips ampersands and percent signs
Exit like kisses.
It is Monday in her mind: morals
Launder and present themselves.
What am I to make of these contradictions?
I wear white cuffs, I bow.
Is this love then, this red material
Issuing from the steele needle that flies so blindingly?
It will make little dresses and coats,
It will cover a dynasty.
How her body opens and shuts --
A Swiss watch, jeweled in the hinges!
O heart, such disorganization!
The stars are flashing like terrible numerals.
ABC, her eyelids say.

Apprehensions

There is this white wall, above which the sky creates itself-
Infinite, green, utterly untouchable.
Angels swim in it, and the stars, in indifference also.
They are my medium.
The sun dissolves on this wall, bleeding its lights.
A grey wall now, clawed and bloody.
Is there no way out of the mind?
Steps at my back spiral into a well.
There are no trees or birds in this world,
There is only sourness.
This red wall winces continually:
A red fist, opening and closing,
Two grey, papery bags-
This is what i am made of, this, and a terror
Of being wheeled off under crosses and rain of pieties.
On a black wall, unidentifiable birds
Swivel their heads and cry.
There is no talk of immorality amoun these!
Cold blanks approach us:
They move in a hurry.

April 18

the slime of all my yesterdays
rots in the hollow of my skull
and if my stomach would contract
because of some explicable phenomenon
such as pregnancy or constipation
I would not remember you
or that because of sleep
infrequent as a moon of greencheese
that because of food
nourishing as violet leaves
that because of these
and in a few fatal yards of grass
in a few spaces of sky and treetops
a future was lost yesterday
as easily and irretrievably
as a tennis ball at twilight

Ariel

Stasis in darkness.
Then the substanceless blue
Pour of tor and distances.
God's lioness,
How one we grow,
Pivot of heels and knees! ---The furrow
Splits and passes, sister to
The brown arc
Of the neck I cannot catch,
Nigger-eye
Berries cast dark
Hooks ---
Black sweet blood mouthfuls,
Shadows.
Something else
Hauls me through air ---
Thighs, hair;
Flakes from my heels.
White
Godiva, I unpeel ---
Dead hands, dead stringencies.
And now I
Foam to wheat, a glitter of seas.
The child's cry
Melts in the wall.
And I
Am the arrow,
The dew that flies,
Suicidal, at one with the drive
Into the red
Eye, the cauldron of morning.

Balloons

Since Christmas they have lived with us,
Guileless and clear,
Oval soul-animals,
Taking up half the space,
Moving and rubbing on the silk
Invisible air drifts,
Giving a shriek and pop
When attacked, then scooting to rest, barely trembling.
Yellow cathead, blue fish--------
Such queer moons we live with
Instead of dead furniture!
Straw mats, white walls
And these traveling
Globes of thin air, red, green,
Delighting
The heart like wishes or free
Peacocks blessing
Old ground with a feather
Beaten in starry metals.
Your small
Brother is making
His balloon squeak like a cat.
Seeming to see
A funny pink world he might eat on the other side of it,
He bites,
Then sits
Back, fat jug
Contemplating a world clear as water.
A red
Shred in his little fist.
5 February 1963

Berck-Plage

(1)

This is the sea, then, this great abeyance.

How the sun's poultice draws on my inflammation.

Electrifyingly-colored sherbets, scooped from the freeze

By pale girls, travel the air in scorched hands.

Why is it so quiet, what are they hiding?

I have two legs, and I move smilingly..

A sandy damper kills the vibrations;

It stretches for miles, the shrunk voices

Waving and crutchless, half their old size.

The lines of the eye, scalded by these bald surfaces,

Boomerang like anchored elastics, hurting the owner.

Is it any wonder he puts on dark glasses?

Is it any wonder he affects a black cassock?

Here he comes now, among the mackerel gatherers

Who wall up their backs against him.

They are handling the black and green lozenges

like the parts of a body.

The sea, that crystallized these,

Creeps away, many-snaked, with a long hiss of distress.

(2)

This black boot has no mercy for anybody.

Why should it, it is the hearse of a dad foot,

The high, dead, toeless foot of this priest

Who plumbs the well of his book,

The bent print bulging before him like scenery.

Obscene bikinis hid in the dunes,

Breasts and hips a confectioner's sugar

Of little crystals, titillating the light,

While a green pool opens its eye,

Sick with what it has swallowed----

Limbs, images, shrieks. Behind the concrete bunkers

Two lovers unstick themselves.

O white sea-crockery,
What cupped sighs, what salt in the throat....

And the onlooker, trembling,
Drawn like a long material
Through a still virulence,
And a weed, hairy as privates.
(3)
On the balconies of the hotel, things are glittering.
Things, things----
Tubular steel wheelchairs, aluminum crutches.
Such salt-sweetness. Why should I walk
Beyond the breakwater, spotty with barnacles?
I am not a nurse, white and attendant,
I am not a smile.
These children are after something, with hooks and cries,
And my heart too small to bandage their terrible faults.
This is the side of a man: his red ribs,
The nerves bursting like trees, and this is the surgeon:
One mirrory eye----
A facet of knowledge.
On a striped mattress in one room
An old man is vanishing.
There is no help in his weeping wife.
Where are the eye-stones, yellow and valuable,
And the tongue, sapphire of ash.
(4)
A wedding-cake face in a paper frill.
How superior he is now.
It is like possessing a saint.
The nurses in their wing-caps are no longer so beautiful;
They are browning, like touched gardenias.
The bed is rolled from the wall.
This is what it is to be complete. It is horrible.
Is he wearing pajamas or an evening suit

Under the glued sheet from which his powdery beak

Rises so whitely unbuffeted?
They propped his jaw with a book until it stiffened
And folded his hands, that were shaking: goodbye, goodbye.
Now the washed sheets fly in the sun,
The pillow cases are sweetening.
It is a blessing, it is a blessing:
The long coffin of soap-colored oak,
The curious bearers and the raw date
Engraving itself in silver with marvelous calm.

(5)

The gray sky lowers, the hills like a green sea
Run fold upon fold far off, concealing their hollows,
The hollows in which rock the thoughts of the wife----
Blunt, practical boats
Full of dresses and hats and china and married daughters.
In the parlor of the stone house
One curtain is flickering from the open window,
Flickering and pouring, a pitiful candle.
This is the tongue of the dead man: remember, remember.
How far he is now, his actions
Around him like living room furniture, like a décor.
As the pallors gather----
The pallors of hands and neighborly faces,
The elate pallors of flying iris.
They are flying off into nothing: remember us.
The empty benches of memory look over stones,
Marble facades with blue veins, and jelly-glassfuls of daffodils.
It is so beautiful up here: it is a stopping place.

(6)

The natural fatness of these lime leaves!----
Pollarded green balls, the trees march to church.
The voice of the priest, in thin air,

Meets the corpse at the gate,
Addressing it, while the hills roll the notes
of the dead bell;
A glitter of wheat and crude earth.

What is the name of that color?----
Old blood of caked walls the sun heals,
Old blood of limb stumps, burnt hearts.
The widow with her black pocketbook and three daughters,
Necessary among the flowers,
Enfolds her lace like fine linen,
Not to be spread again.
While a sky, wormy with put-by smiles,
Passes cloud after cloud.
And the bride flowers expend a freshness,
And the soul is a bride
In a still place, and the groom is red and forgetful, he is featureless.
(7)
Behind the glass of this car
The world purrs, shut-off and gentle.
And I am dark-suited and still, a member of the party,
Gliding up in low gear behind the cart.
And the priest is a vessel,
A tarred fabric, sorry and dull,
Following the coffin on its flowery cart like a beautiful woman,
A crest of breasts, eyelids and lips
Storming the hilltop.
Then, from the barred yard, the children
Smell the melt of shoe-blacking,
Their faces turning, wordless and slow,
Their eyes opening
On a wonderful thing----
Six round black hats in the grass and a lozenge of wood,
And a naked mouth, red and awkward.
For a minute the sky pours into the hole like plasma.
There is no hope, it is given up.

Black Rook in Rainy Weather

On the stiff twig up there
Hunches a wet black rook
Arranging and rearranging its feathers in the rain-
I do not expect a miracle
Or an accident

To set the sight on fire
In my eye, nor seek
Any more in the desultory weather some design,
But let spotted leaves fall as they fall
Without ceremony, or portent.

Although, I admit, I desire,
Occasionally, some backtalk
From the mute sky, I can't honestly complain:
A certain minor light may still
Lean incandescent

Out of kitchen table or chair
As if a celestial burning took
Possession of the most obtuse objects now and then --
Thus hallowing an interval
Otherwise inconsequent

By bestowing largesse, honor
One might say love. At any rate, I now walk
Wary (for it could happen
Even in this dull, ruinous landscape); sceptical
Yet politic, ignorant

Of whatever angel any choose to flare
Suddenly at my elbow. I only know that a rook
Ordering its black feathers can so shine
As to seize my senses, haul
My eyelids up, and grant

A brief respite from fear
Of total neutrality. With luck,
Trekking stubborn through this season

Of fatigue, I shall
Patch together a content
Of sorts. Miracles occur.
If you care to call those spasmodic
Tricks of radiance
Miracles. The wait's begun again,
The long wait for the angel,
For that rare, random descent.

Blackberrying

Nobody in the lane, and nothing, nothing but blackberries,
Blackberries on either side, though on the right mainly,
A blackberry alley, going down in hooks, and a sea
Somewhere at the end of it, heaving. Blackberries
Big as the ball of my thumb, and dumb as eyes
Ebon in the hedges, fat
With blue-red juices. These they squander on my fingers.
I had not asked for such a blood sisterhood; they must love me.
They accommodate themselves to my milkbottle, flattening their
sides.

Overhead go the choughs in black, cacophonous flocks ---
Bits of burnt paper wheeling in a blown sky.
Theirs is the only voice, protesting, protesting.
I do not think the sea will appear at all.
The high, green meadows are glowing, as if lit from within.
I come to one bush of berries so ripe it is a bush of flies,
Hanging their bluegreen bellies and their wing panes in a Chinese
screen.
The honey-feast of the berries has stunned them; they believe in
heaven.
One more hook, and the berries and bushes end.
The only thing to come now is the sea.
From between two hills a sudden wind funnels at me,
Slapping its phantom laundry in my face.
These hills are too green and sweet to have tasted salt.
I follow the sheep path between them.
A last hook brings me
To the hills' northern face, and the face is orange rock
That looks out on nothing, nothing
but a great space
Of white and pewter lights, and
a din like silversmiths
Beating and beating at an intractable metal.

Bucolics

Mayday: two came to field in such wise :
`A daisied mead', each said to each,
So were they one; so sought they couch,
Across barbed stile, through flocked brown cows.
`No pitchforked farmer, please,' she said;
`May cockcrow guard us safe,' said he;
By blackthorn thicket, flower spray
They pitched their coats, come to green bed.
Below: a fen where water stood;
Aslant: their hill of stinging nettle;
Then, honor-bound, mute grazing cattle;
Above: leaf-wraithed white air, white cloud.
All afternoon these lovers lay
Until the sun turned pale from warm,
Until sweet wind changed tune, blew harm :
Cruel nettles stung her angles raw.
Rueful, most vexed, that tender skin
Should accept so fell a wound,
He stamped and cracked stalks to the ground
Which had caused his dear girl pain.
Now he goes from his rightful road
And, under honor, will depart;
While she stands burning, venom-girt,
In wait for sharper smart to fade.

By Candlelight

This is winter, this is night, small love --
A sort of black horsehair,
A rough, dumb country stuff
Steeled with the sheen
Of what green stars can make it to our gate.
I hold you on my arm.
It is very late.
The dull bells tongue the hour.
The mirror floats us at one candle power.
This is the fluid in which we meet each other,
This haloey radiance that seems to breathe
And lets our shadows wither
Only to blow
Them huge again, violent giants on the wall.
One match scratch makes you real.
At first the candle will not bloom at all --
It snuffs its bud
To almost nothing, to a dull blue dud.
I hold my breath until you creak to life,
Balled hedgehog,
Small and cross. The yellow knife
Grows tall. You clutch your bars.
My singing makes you roar.
I rock you like a boat
Across the Indian carpet, the cold floor,
While the brass man
Kneels, back bent, as best he can
Hefting his white pillar with the light
That keeps the sky at bay,
The sack of black! It is everywhere, tight, tight!
He is yours, the little brassy Atlas --
Poor heirloom, all you have,
At his heels a pile of five brass cannonballs,

No child, no wife.
Five balls! Five bright brass balls!
To juggle with, my love, when the sky falls.

Child

Your clear eye is the one absolutely beautiful thing.
I want to fill it with color and ducks,
The zoo of the new

Whose name you meditate --
April snowdrop, Indian pipe,
Little

Stalk without wrinkle,
Pool in which images
Should be grand and classical

Not this troublous
Wringing of hands, this dark
Ceiling without a star.

Cinderella

The prince leans to the girl in scarlet heels,
Her green eyes slant, hair flaring in a fan
Of silver as the rondo slows; now reels
Begin on tilted violins to span
The whole revolving tall glass palace hall
Where guests slide gliding into light like wine;
Rose candles flicker on the lilac wall
Reflecting in a million flagons' shine,
And glided couples all in whirling trance
Follow holiday revel begun long since,
Until near twelve the strange girl all at once
Guilt-stricken halts, pales, clings to the prince
As amid the hectic music and cocktail talk
She hears the caustic ticking of the clock.

Contusion

Color floods to the spot, dull purple.
The rest of the body is all washed-out,
The color of pearl.
In a pit of a rock
The sea sucks obsessively,
One hollow thw whole sea's pivot.
The size of a fly,
The doom mark
Crawls down the wall.
The heart shuts,
The sea slides back,
The mirrors are sheeted.

Conversation Among the Ruins

Through portico of my elegant house you stalk
With your wild furies, disturbing garlands of fruit
And the fabulous lutes and peacocks, rending the net
Of all decorum which holds the whirlwind back.
Now, rich order of walls is fallen; rooks croak
Above the appalling ruin; in bleak light
Of your stormy eye, magic takes flight
Like a daunted witch, quitting castle when real days break.
Fractured pillars frame prospects of rock;
While you stand heroic in coat and tie, I sit
Composed in Grecian tunic and psyche-knot,
Rooted to your black look, the play turned tragic:
Which such blight wrought on our bankrupt estate,
What ceremony of words can patch the havoc?

Crossing the River

Black lake, black boat, two black, cut-paper people.
Where do the black trees go that drink here?
Their shadows must cover Canada.
A little light is filtering from the water flowers.
Their leaves do not wish us to hurry:
They are round and flat and full of dark advice.
Cold worlds shake from the oar.
The spirit of blackness is in us, it is in the fishes.
A snag is lifting a valedictory, pale hand;
Stars open among the lilies.
Are you not blinded by such expressionless sirens?
This is the silence of astounded souls.

Crossing The Water

Black lake, black boat, two black, cut-paper people.
Where do the black trees go that drink here?
Their shadows must cover Canada.
A little light is filtering from the water flowers.
Their leaves do not wish us to hurry:
They are round and flat and full of dark advice.
Cold worlds shake from the oar.
The spirit of blackness is in us, it is in the fishes.
A snag is lifting a valedictory, pale hand;
Stars open among the lilies.
Are you not blinded by such expressionless sirens?
This is the silence of astounded souls.

Cut

What a thrill -
My thumb instead of an onion.
The top quite gone
Except for a sort of hinge
Of skin,
A flap like a hat,
Dead white.
Then that red plush.
Little pilgrim,
The Indian's axed your scalp.
Your turkey wattle
Carpet rolls
Straight from the heart.
I step on it,
Clutching my bottle
Of pink fizz. A celebration, this is.
Out of a gap
A million soldiers run,
Redcoats, every one.
Whose side are they one?
O my
Homunculus, I am ill.
I have taken a pill to kill
The thin
Papery feeling.
Saboteur,
Kamikaze man -
The stain on your
Gauze Ku Klux Klan
Babushka
Darkens and tarnishes and when
The balled
Pulp of your heart

Confronts its small
Mill of silence
How you jump -
Trepanned veteran,
Dirty girl,
Thumb stump.

Daddy

You do not do, you do not do
Any more, black shoe
In which I have lived like a foot
For thirty years, poor and white,
Barely daring to breathe or Achoo.

Daddy, I have had to kill you.
You died before I had time---
Marble-heavy, a bag full of God,
Ghastly statue with one gray toe
Big as a Frisco seal

And a head in the freakish Atlantic
Where it pours bean green over blue
In the waters off the beautiful Nauset.
I used to pray to recover you.
Ach, du.

In the German tongue, in the Polish town
Scraped flat by the roller
Of wars, wars, wars.
But the name of the town is common.
My Polack friend

Says there are a dozen or two.
So I never could tell where you
Put your foot, your root,
I never could talk to you.
The tongue stuck in my jaw.

It stuck in a barb wire snare.
Ich, ich, ich, ich,
I could hardly speak.
I thought every German was you.
And the language obscene

An engine, an engine,
Chuffing me off like a Jew.
A Jew to Dachau, Auschwitz, Belsen.

I began to talk like a Jew.
I think I may well be a Jew.
The snows of the Tyrol, the clear beer of Vienna
Are not very pure or true.
With my gypsy ancestress and my weird luck
And my Taroc pack and my Taroc pack
I may be a bit of a Jew.
I have always been scared of you,
With your Luftwaffe, your gobbledygoo.
And your neat mustache
And your Aryan eye, bright blue.

Panzer-man, panzer-man, O You----
Not God but a swastika
So black no sky could squeak through.
Every woman adores a Fascist,
The boot in the face, the brute
Brute heart of a brute like you.
You stand at the blackboard, daddy,
In the picture I have of you,
A cleft in your chin instead of your foot
But no less a devil for that, no not
Any less the black man who
Bit my pretty red heart in two.
I was ten when they buried you.
At twenty I tried to die
And get back, back, back to you.
I thought even the bones would do.
But they pulled me out of the sack,
And they stuck me together with glue.
And then I knew what to do.
I made a model of you,
A man in black with a Meinkampf look
And a love of the rack and the screw.
And I said I do, I do.
So daddy, I'm finally through.
The black telephone's off at the root,

The voices just can't worm through.
If I've killed one man, I've killed two---
The vampire who said he was you
And drank my blood for a year,
Seven years, if you want to know.
Daddy, you can lie back now.
There's a stake in your fat black heart
And the villagersnever liked you.
They are dancing and stamping on you.
They always knew it was you.
Daddy, daddy, you bastard, I'm through.

Death & Co.

Two, of course there are two.
It seems perfectly natural now ----
The one who never looks up, whose eyes are lidded
And balled, like Blake's.
Who exhibits
The birthmarks that are his trademark ----
The scald scar of water,
The nude
Verdigris of the condor.
I am red meat. His beak
Claps sidewise: I am not his yet.
He tells me how badly I photograph.
He tells me how sweet
The babies look in their hospital
Icebox, a simple
Frill at the neck
Then the flutings of their Ionian
Death-gowns.
Then two little feet.
He does not smile or smoke.
The other does that
His hair long and plausive
Bastard
Masturbating a glitter
He wants to be loved.
I do not stir.
The frost makes a flower,
The dew makes a star,
The dead bell,
The dead bell.
Somebody's done for.

Death & Co.

Two, of course there are two.
It seems perfectly natural now——
The one who never looks up, whose eyes are lidded
And balled, like Blake's.
Who exhibits
The birthmarks that are his trademark——
The scald scar of water,
The nude
Verdigris of the condor.
I am red meat. His beak
Claps sidewise: I am not his yet.
He tells me how badly I photograph.
He tells me how sweet
The babies look in their hospital
Icebox, a simple
Frill at the neck
Then the flutings of their Ionian
Death-gowns.
Then two little feet.
He does not smile or smoke.
The other does that
His hair long and plausive
Bastard
Masturbating a glitter
He wants to be loved.
I do not stir.
The frost makes a flower,
The dew makes a star,
The dead bell,
The dead bell.
Somebody's done for.

Dialogue Between Ghost and Priest

In the rectory garden on his evening walk
Paced brisk Father Shawn. A cold day, a sodden one it was
In black November. After a sliding rain
Dew stood in chill sweat on each stalk,
Each thorn; spiring from wet earth, a blue haze
Hung caught in dark-webbed branches like a fabulous heron.
Hauled sudden from solitude,
Hair prickling on his head,
Father Shawn perceived a ghost
Shaping itself from that mist.
'How now,' Father Shawn crisply addressed the ghost
Wavering there, gauze-edged, smelling of woodsmoke,
'What manner of business are you on?
From your blue pallor, I'd say you inhabited the frozen waste
Of hell, and not the fiery part. Yet to judge by that dazzled look,
That noble mien, perhaps you've late quitted heaven?'
In voice furred with frost,
Ghost said to priest:
'Neither of those countries do I frequent:
Earth is my haunt.'
'Come, come,' Father Shawn gave an impatient shrug,
'I don't ask you to spin some ridiculous fable
Of gilded harps or gnawing fire: simply tell
After your life's end, what just epilogue
God ordained to follow up your days. Is it such trouble
To satisfy the questions of a curious old fool?'
'In life, love gnawed my skin
To this white bone;
What love did then, love does now:
Gnaws me through.'
'What love,' asked Father Shawn, 'but too great love
Of flawed earth-flesh could cause this sorry pass?
Some damned condition you are in:
Thinking never to have left the world, you grieve

As though alive, shriveling in torment thus
To atone as shade for sin that lured blind man.'
'The day of doom
Is not yest come.
Until that time
A crock of dust is my dear hom.'
'Fond phantom,' cried shocked Father Shawn,
'Can there be such stubbornness--
A soul grown feverish, clutching its dead body-tree
Like a last storm-crossed leaf? Best get you gone

To judgment in a higher court of grace.
Repent, depart, before God's trump-crack splits the sky.'
From that pale mist
Ghost swore to priest:
'There sits no higher court
Than man's red heart.'

Edge

The woman is perfected
Her dead
Body wears the smile of accomplishment,
The illusion of a Greek necessity
Flows in the scrolls of her toga,
Her bare
Feet seem to be saying:
We have come so far, it is over.
Each dead child coiled, a white serpent,
One at each little
Pitcher of milk, now empty
She has folded
Them back into her body as petals
Of a rose close when the garden
Stiffens and odors bleed
From the sweet, deep throats of the night flower.
The moon has nothing to be sad about,
Staring from her hood of bone.
She is used to this sort of thing.
Her blacks crackle and drag.

Electra on Azalea Path

The day you died I went into the dirt,
Into the lightless hibernaculum
Where bees, striped black and gold, sleep out the blizzard
Like hieratic stones, and the ground is hard.
It was good for twenty years, that wintering --
As if you never existed, as if I came
God-fathered into the world from my mother's belly:
Her wide bed wore the stain of divinity.
I had nothing to do with guilt or anything
When I wormed back under my mother's heart.
Small as a doll in my dress of innocence
I lay dreaming your epic, image by image.
Nobody died or withered on that stage.
Everything took place in a durable whiteness.
The day I woke, I woke on Churchyard Hill.
I found your name, I found your bones and all
Enlisted in a cramped necropolis
your speckled stone skewed by an iron fence.
In this charity ward, this poorhouse, where the dead
Crowd foot to foot, head to head, no flower
Breaks the soil. This is Azalea path.
A field of burdock opens to the south.
Six feet of yellow gravel cover you.
The artificial red sage does not stir
In the basket of plastic evergreens they put
At the headstone next to yours, nor does it rot,
Although the rains dissolve a bloody dye:
The ersatz petals drip, and they drip red.
Another kind of redness bothers me:
The day your slack sail drank my sister's breath
The flat sea purpled like that evil cloth
My mother unrolled at your last homecoming.
I borrow the silts of an old tragedy.

The truth is, one late October, at my birth-cry
A scorpion stung its head, an ill-starred thing;
My mother dreamed you face down in the sea.
The stony actors poise and pause for breath.
I brought my love to bear, and then you died.
It was the gangrene ate you to the bone
My mother said: you died like any man.
How shall I age into that state of mind?
I am the ghost of an infamous suicide,
My own blue razor rusting at my throat.
O pardon the one who knocks for pardon at
Your gate, father -- your hound-bitch, daughter, friend.
It was my love that did us both to death.

Elm

I know the bottom, she says. I know it with my great tap root;
It is what you fear.
I do not fear it: I have been there.

Is it the sea you hear in me,
Its dissatisfactions?
Or the voice of nothing, that was you madness?

Love is a shadow.
How you lie and cry after it.
Listen: these are its hooves: it has gone off, like a horse.

All night I shall gallup thus, impetuously,
Till your head is a stone, your pillow a little turf,
Echoing, echoing.

Or shall I bring you the sound of poisons?
This is rain now, the big hush.
And this is the fruit of it: tin white, like arsenic.

I have suffered the atrocity of sunsets.
Scorched to the root
My red filaments burn and stand,a hand of wires.

Now I break up in pieces that fly about like clubs.
A wind of such violence
Will tolerate no bystanding: I must shriek.

The moon, also, is merciless: she would drag me
Cruelly, being barren.
Her radiance scathes me. Or perhaps I have caught her.

I let her go. I let her go
Diminished and flat, as after radical surgery.
How your bad dreams possess and endow me.

I am inhabited by a cry.
Nightly it flaps out
Looking, with its hooks, for something to love.

I am terrified by this dark thing
That sleeps in me;
All day I feel its soft, feathery turnings, its malignity.

Clouds pass and disperse.
Are those the faces of love, those pale irretrievables?
Is it for such I agitate my heart?
I am incapable of more knowledge.
What is this, this face
So murderous in its strangle of branches?--

Its snaky acids kiss.
It petrifies the will. These are the isolate, slow faults
That kill, that kill, that kill.

Face Lift

You bring me good news from the clinic,
Whipping off your silk scarf, exhibiting the tight white
Mummy-cloths, smiling: I'm all right.
When I was nine, a lime-green anesthetist
Fed me banana-gas through a frog mask. The nauseous vault
Boomed with bad dreams and the Jovian voices of surgeons.
Then mother swam up, holding a tin basin.
O I was sick.

They've changed all that. Traveling
Nude as Cleopatra in my well-boiled hospital shift,
Fizzy with sedatives and unusually humorous,
I roll to an anteroom where a kind man
Fists my fingers for me. He makes me feel something precious
Is leaking from the finger-vents. At the count of two,
Darkness wipes me out like chalk on a blackboard. . .
I don't know a thing.

For five days I lie in secret,
Tapped like a cask, the years draining into my pillow.
Even my best friend thinks I'm in the country.
Skin doesn't have roots, it peels away easy as paper.
When I grin, the stitches tauten. I grow backward. I'm twenty,
Broody and in long skirts on my first husband's sofa, my fingers
Buried in the lambswool of the dead poodle;
I hadn't a cat yet.

Now she's done for, the dewlapped lady
I watched settle, line by line, in my mirror—
Old sock-face, sagged on a darning egg.
They've trapped her in some laboratory jar.
Let her die there, or wither incessantly
for the next fifty years,
Nodding and rocking and fingering her thin hair.
Mother to myself, I wake swaddled in gauze,
Pink and smooth as a baby.

Faun

Haunched like a faun, he hooed
From grove of moon-glint and fen-frost
Until all owls in the twigged forest
Flapped black to look and brood
On the call this man made.
No sound but a drunken coot
Lurching home along river bank.
Stars hung water-sunk, so a rank
Of double star-eyes lit
Boughs where those owls sat.
An arena of yellow eyes
Watched the changing shape he cut,
Saw hoof harden from foot, saw sprout
Goat-horns. Marked how god rose
And galloped woodward in that guise.

Fever 103 deg.

Pure? What does it mean?
The tongues of hell
Are dull, dull as the triple
Tongues of dull, fat Cerebus
Who wheezes at the gate. Incapable
Of licking clean
The aguey tendon, the sin, the sin.
The tinder cries.
The indelible smell
Of a snuffed candle!
Love, love, the low smokes roll
From me like Isadora's scarves, I'm in a fright
One scarf will catch and anchor in the wheel.
Such yellow sullen smokes
Make their own element. They will not rise,
But trundle round the globe
Choking the aged and the meek,
The weak
Hothouse baby in its crib,
The ghastly orchid
Hanging its hanging garden in the air,
Devilish leopard!
Radiation turned it white
And killed it in an hour.
Greasing the bodies of adulterers
Like Hiroshima ash and eating in.
The sin. The sin.
Darling, all night
I have been flickering, off, on, off, on.
The sheets grow heavy as a lecher's kiss.
Three days. Three nights.
Lemon water, chicken
Water, water make me retch.

I am too pure for you or anyone.
Your body
Hurts me as the world hurts God. I am a lantern--
My head a moon
Of Japanese paper, my gold beaten skin
Infinitely delicate and infinitely expensive.

Does not my heat astound you. And my light.
All by myself I am a huge camellia
Glowing and coming and going, flush on flush.
I think I am going up,
I think I may rise--
The beads of hot metal fly, and I, love, I
Am a pure acetylene
Virgin
Attended by roses,
By kisses, by cherubim,
By whatever these pink things mean.
Not you, nor him.
Not him, nor him
(My selves dissolving, old whore petticoats)--
To Paradise.

Fever 103°

Pure? What does it mean?
The tongues of hell
Are dull, dull as the triple
Tongues of dull, fat Cerebus
Who wheezes at the gate. Incapable
Of licking clean
The aguey tendon, the sin, the sin.
The tinder cries.
The indelible smell
Of a snuffed candle!
Love, love, the low smokes roll
From me like Isadora's scarves, I'm in a fright
One scarf will catch and anchor in the wheel.
Such yellow sullen smokes
Make their own element. They will not rise,
But trundle round the globe
Choking the aged and the meek,
The weak
Hothouse baby in its crib,
The ghastly orchid
Hanging its hanging garden in the air,
Devilish leopard!
Radiation turned it white
And killed it in an hour.
Greasing the bodies of adulterers
Like Hiroshima ash and eating in.
The sin. The sin.
Darling, all night
I have been flickering, off, on, off, on.
The sheets grow heavy as a lecher's kiss.
Three days. Three nights.
Lemon water, chicken
Water, water make me retch.

I am too pure for you or anyone.
Your body
Hurts me as the world hurts God. I am a lantern ----
My head a moon
Of Japanese paper, my gold beaten skin
Infinitely delicate and infinitely expensive.

Does not my heat astound you. And my light.
All by myself I am a huge camellia
Glowing and coming and going, flush on flush.
I think I am going up,
I think I may rise ----
The beads of hot metal fly, and I, love, I
Am a pure acetylene
Virgin
Attended by roses,
By kisses, by cherubim,
By whatever these pink things mean.
Not you, nor him.
Not him, nor him
(My selves dissolving, old whore petticoats) ----
To Paradise.

Fiesta Melons

In Benidorm there are melons,
Whole donkey-carts full
Of innumerable melons,
Ovals and balls,
Bright green and thumpable
Laced over with stripes
Of turtle-dark green.
Chooose an egg-shape, a world-shape,
Bowl one homeward to taste
In the whitehot noon :
Cream-smooth honeydews,
Pink-pulped whoppers,
Bump-rinded cantaloupes
With orange cores.
Each wedge wears a studding
Of blanched seeds or black seeds
To strew like confetti
Under the feet of
This market of melon-eating
Fiesta-goers.

Full Fathom Five

Old man, you surface seldom.
Then you come in with the tide's coming
When seas wash cold, foam-
Capped: white hair, white beard, far-flung,
A dragnet, rising, falling, as waves
Crest and trough. Miles long
Extend the radial sheaves
Of your spread hair, in which wrinkling skeins
Knotted, caught, survives
The old myth of orgins
Unimaginable. You float near
As kneeled ice-mountains
Of the north, to be steered clear
Of, not fathomed. All obscurity
Starts with a danger:
Your dangers are many. I
Cannot look much but your form suffers
Some strange injury
And seems to die: so vapors
Ravel to clearness on the dawn sea.
The muddy rumors
Of your burial move me
To half-believe: your reappearance
Proves rumors shallow,
For the archaic trenched lines
Of your grained face shed time in runnels:
Ages beat like rains
On the unbeaten channels
Of the ocean. Such sage humor and
Durance are whirlpools
To make away with the ground-
Work of the earth and the sky's ridgepole.
Waist down, you may wind

One labyrinthine tangle
To root deep among knuckles, shinbones,
Skulls. Inscrutable,
Below shoulders not once
Seen by any man who kept his head,
You defy questions;

You defy godhood.
I walk dry on your kingdom's border
Exiled to no good.
Your shelled bed I remember.
Father, this thick air is murderous.
I would breathe water.

Getting There

How far is it?
How far is it now?
The gigantic gorilla interior
Of the wheels move, they appall me ---
The terrible brains
Of Krupp, black muzzles
Revolving, the sound
Punching out Absence! Like cannon.
It is Russia I have to get across, it is some was or other.
I am dragging my body
Quietly through the straw of the boxcars.
Now is the time for bribery.
What do wheels eat, these wheels
Fixed to their arcs like gods,
The silver leash of the will ----
Inexorable. And their pride!
All the gods know destinations.
I am a letter in this slot!
I fly to a name, two eyes.
Will there be fire, will there be bread?
Here there is such mud.
It is a trainstop, the nurses
Undergoing the faucet water, its veils, veils in a nunnery,
Touching their wounded,
The men the blood still pumps forward,
Legs, arms piled outside
The tent of unending cries ----
A hospital of dolls.
And the men, what is left of the men
Pumped ahead by these pistons, this blood
Into the next mile,
The next hour ----
Dynasty of broken arrows!

How far is it?
There is mud on my feet,
Thick, red and slipping. It is Adam's side,
This earth I rise from, and I in agony.
I cannot undo myself, and the train is steaming.
Steaming and breathing, its teeth
Ready to roll, like a devil's.
There is a minute at the end of it
A minute, a dewdrop.
How far is it?
It is so small
The place I am getting to, why are there these obstacles ----
The body of this woman,
Charred skirts and deathmask
Mourned by religious figures, by garlanded children.
And now detonations ----
Thunder and guns.
The fire's between us.

Is there no place
Turning and turning in the middle air,
Untouchable and untouchable.
The train is dragging itself, it is screaming ----
An animal
Insane for the destination,
The bloodspot,
The face at the end of the flare.
I shall bury the wounded like pupas,
I shall count and bury the dead.
Let their souls writhe in like dew,
Incense in my track.
The carriages rock, they are cradles.
And I, stepping from this skin
Of old bandages, boredoms, old faces
Step up to you from the black car of Lethe,
Pure as a baby.

Gigolo

Pocket watch, I tick well.
The streets are lizardly crevices
Sheer-sided, with holes where to hide.
It is best to meet in a cul-de-sac,
A palace of velvet
With windows of mirrors.
There one is safe,
There are no family photographs,
No rings through the nose, no cries.
Bright fish hooks, the smiles of women
Gulp at my bulk
And I, in my snazzy blacks,
Mill a litter of breasts like jellyfish.
To nourish
The cellos of moans I eat eggs --
Eggs and fish, the essentials,
The aphrodisiac squid.
My mouth sags,
The mouth of Christ
When my engine reaches the end of it.
The tattle of my
Gold joints, my way of turning
Bitches to ripples of silver
Rolls out a carpet, a hush.
And there is no end, no end of it.
I shall never grow old. New oysters
Shriek in the sea and I
Glitter like Fontainebleu
Gratified,
All the fall of water an eye
Over whose pool I tenderly
Lean and see me.

Goatsucker

Old goatherds swear how all night long they hear
The warning whirr and burring of the bird
Who wakes with darkness and till dawn works hard
Vampiring dry of milk each great goat udder.
Moon full, moon dark, the chary dairy farmer
Dreams that his fattest cattle dwindle, fevered
By claw-cuts of the Goatsucker, alias Devil-bird,
Its eye, flashlit, a chip of ruby fire.
So fables say the Goatsucker moves, masked from men's sight
In an ebony air, on wings of witch cloth,
Well-named, ill-famed a knavish fly-by-night,
Yet it never milked any goat, nor dealt cow death
And shadows only--cave-mouth bristle beset--
Cockchafers and the wan, green luna moth.

I Am Vertical

But I would rather be horizontal.
I am not a tree with my root in the soil
Sucking up minerals and motherly love
So that each March I may gleam into leaf,
Nor am I the beauty of a garden bed
Attracting my share of Ahs and spectacularly painted,
Unknowing I must soon unpetal.
Compared with me, a tree is immortal
And a flower-head not tall, but more startling,
And I want the one's longevity and the other's daring.
Tonight, in the infinitesimal light of the stars,
The trees and flowers have been strewing their cool odors.
I walk among them, but none of them are noticing.
Sometimes I think that when I am sleeping
I must most perfectly resemble them--
Thoughts gone dim.
It is more natural to me, lying down.
Then the sky and I are in open conversation,
And I shall be useful when I lie down finally:
The the trees may touch me for once, and the flowers have time for
me.

In Plaster

I shall never get out of this! There are two of me now:
This new absolutely white person and the old yellow one,
And the white person is certainly the superior one.
She doesn't need food, she is one of the real saints.
At the beginning I hated her, she had no personality --
She lay in bed with me like a dead body
And I was scared, because she was shaped just the way I was
Only much whiter and unbreakable and with no complaints.
I couldn't sleep for a week, she was so cold.
I blamed her for everything, but she didn't answer.
I couldn't understand her stupid behavior!
When I hit her she held still, like a true pacifist.
Then I realized what she wanted was for me to love her:
She began to warm up, and I saw her advantages.
Without me, she wouldn't exist, so of course she was grateful.
I gave her a soul, I bloomed out of her as a rose
Blooms out of a vase of not very valuable porcelain,
And it was I who attracted everybody's attention,
Not her whiteness and beauty, as I had at first supposed.
I patronized her a little, and she lapped it up --
You could tell almost at once she had a slave mentality.
I didn't mind her waiting on me, and she adored it.
In the morning she woke me early, reflecting the sun
From her amazingly white torso, and I couldn't help but notice
Her tidiness and her calmness and her patience:
She humored my weakness like the best of nurses,
Holding my bones in place so they
would mend properly.
In time our relationship grew more intense.
She stopped fitting me so closely and seemed offish.
I felt her criticizing me in spite of herself,
As if my habits offended her in some way.
She let in the drafts and became more

and more absent-minded.
And my skin itched and flaked away in soft pieces
Simply because she looked after me so badly.
Then I saw what the trouble was: she thought she was immortal.
She wanted to leave me, she thought she was superior,
And I'd been keeping her in the dark, and she was resentful --
Wasting her days waiting on a half-corpse!
And secretly she began to hope I'd die.
Then she could cover my mouth and eyes, cover me entirely,
And wear my painted face the way a mummy-case
Wears the face of a pharaoh, though it's made of mud and water.
I wasn't in any position to get rid of her.
She'd supported me for so long I was quite limp --
I had forgotten how to walk or sit,
So I was careful not to upset her in any way

Or brag ahead of time how I'd avenge myself.
Living with her was like living with my own coffin:
Yet I still depended on her, though I did it regretfully.
I used to think we might make a go of it together --
After all, it was a kind of marriage, being so close.
Now I see it must be one or the other of us.
She may be a saint, and I may be ugly and hairy,
But she'll soon find out that that doesn't matter a bit.
I'm collecting my strength; one day I shall manage without her,
And she'll perish with emptiness then, and begin to miss me.

Insomniac

The night is only a sort of carbon paper,
Blueblack, with the much-poked periods of stars
Letting in the light, peephole after peephole . . .
A bonewhite light, like death, behind all things.
Under the eyes of the stars and the moon's rictus
He suffers his desert pillow, sleeplessness
Stretching its fine, irritating sand in all directions.
Over and over the old, granular movie
Exposes embarrassments--the mizzling days
Of childhood and adolescence, sticky with dreams,
Parental faces on tall stalks, alternately stern and tearful,
A garden of buggy rose that made him cry.
His forehead is bumpy as a sack of rocks.
Memories jostle each other for face-room like obsolete film stars.
He is immune to pills: red, purple, blue . . .
How they lit the tedium of the protracted evening!
Those sugary planets whose influence won for him
A life baptized in no-life for a while,
And the sweet, drugged waking of a forgetful baby.
Now the pills are worn-out and silly, like classical gods.
Their poppy-sleepy colors do him no good.
His head is a little interior of grey mirrors.
Each gesture flees immediately down an alley
Of diminishing perspectives, and its significance
Drains like water out the hole at the far end.
He lives without privacy in a lidless room,
The bald slots of his eyes stiffened wide-open
On the incessant heat-lightning flicker of situations.
Nightlong, in the granite yard, invisible cats
Have been howling like women, or
damaged instruments.
Already he can feel daylight, his white disease,
Creeping up with her hatful of trivial repetitions.

The city is a map of cheerful twitters now,
And everywhere people, eyes mica-silver and blank,
Are riding to work in rows, as if recently brainwashed.

Jilted

My thoughts are crabbed and sallow,
My tears like vinegar,
Or the bitter blinking yellow
Of an acetic star.
Tonight the caustic wind, love,
Gossips late and soon,
And I wear the wry-faced pucker of
The sour lemon moon.
While like an early summer plum,
Puny, green, and tart,
Droops upon its wizened stem
My lean, unripened heart.

Kindness

Kindness glides about my house.
Dame Kindness, she is so nice!
The blue and red jewels of her rings smoke
In the windows, the mirrors
Are filling with smiles.
What is so real as the cry of a child?
A rabbit's cry may be wilder
But it has no soul.
Sugar can cure everything, so Kindness says.
Sugar is a necessary fluid,
Its crystals a little poultice.
O kindness, kindness
Sweetly picking up pieces!
My Japanese silks, desperate butterflies,
May be pinned any minute, anesthetized.
And here you come, with a cup of tea
Wreathed in steam.
The blood jet is poetry,
There is no stopping it.
You hand me two children, two roses.

Lady Lazarus

I have done it again.
One year in every ten
I manage it----
A sort of walking miracle, my skin
Bright as a Nazi lampshade,
My right foot
A paperweight,
My face a featureless, fine
Jew linen.
Peel off the napkin
0 my enemy.
Do I terrify?----
The nose, the eye pits, the full set of teeth?
The sour breath
Will vanish in a day.
Soon, soon the flesh
The grave cave ate will be
At home on me
And I a smiling woman.
I am only thirty.
And like the cat I have nine times to die.
This is Number Three.
What a trash
To annihilate each decade.
What a million filaments.
The peanut-crunching crowd
Shoves in to see
Them unwrap me hand and foot
The big strip tease.
Gentlemen, ladies
These are my hands
My knees.
I may be skin and bone,

Nevertheless, I am the same, identical woman.
The first time it happened I was ten.
It was an accident.
The second time I meant
To last it out and not come back at all.
I rocked shut

As a seashell.
They had to call and call
And pick the worms off me like sticky pearls.
Dying
Is an art, like everything else,
I do it exceptionally well.
I do it so it feels like hell.
I do it so it feels real.
I guess you could say I've a call.
It's easy enough to do it in a cell.
It's easy enough to do it and stay put.
It's the theatrical
Comeback in broad day
To the same place, the same face, the same brute
Amused shout:
'A miracle!'
That knocks me out.
There is a charge

For the eyeing of my scars, there is a charge
For the hearing of my heart----
It really goes.
And there is a charge, a very large charge
For a word or a touch
Or a bit of blood
Or a piece of my hair or my clothes.
So, so, Herr Doktor.
So, Herr Enemy.
I am your opus,
I am your valuable,
The pure gold baby
That melts to a shriek.

I turn and burn.
Do not think I underestimate your great concern.
Ash, ash ---
You poke and stir.
Flesh, bone, there is nothing there----
A cake of soap,
A wedding ring,
A gold filling.

Herr God, Herr Lucifer

Beware
Beware.
Out of the ash
I rise with my red hair
And I eat men like air.

Landowners

From my rented attic with no earth
To call my own except the air-motes,
I malign the leaden perspective
Of identical gray brick houses,
Orange roof-tiles, orange chimney pots,
And see that first house, as if between
Mirrors, engendering a spectral
Corridor of inane replicas,
Flimsily peopled.
But landowners
Own thier cabbage roots, a space of stars,
Indigenous peace. Such substance makes
My eyeful of reflections a ghost's
Eyeful, which, envious,would define
Death as striking root on one land-tract;
Life, its own vaporous wayfarings.

Last Words

I do not want a plain box, I want a sarcophagus
With tigery stripes, and a face on it
Round as the moon, to stare up.
I want to be looking at them when they come
Picking among the dumb minerals, the roots.
I see them already -- the pale, star-distance faces.
Now they are nothing, they are not even babies.
I imagine them without fathers or mothers, like the first gods.
They will wonder if I was important.
I should sugar and preserve my days like fruit!
My mirror is clouding over --
A few more breaths, and it will reflect nothing at all.
The flowers and the faces whiten to a sheet.
I do not trust the spirit. It escapes like steam
In dreams, through mouth-hole or eye-hole. I can't stop it.
One day it won't come back. Things aren't like that.
They stay, their little particular lusters
Warmed by much handling. They almost purr.
When the soles of my feet grow cold,
The blue eye of my tortoise will comfort me.
Let me have my copper cooking pots, let my rouge pots
Bloom about me like night flowers, with a good smell.
They will roll me up in bandages, they will store my heart
Under my feet in a neat parcel.
I shall hardly know myself. It will be dark,
And the shine of these small things sweeter than the face of Ishtar.

Leaving Early

Lady, your room is lousy with flowers.
When you kick me out, that's what I'll remember,
Me, sitting here bored as a loepard
In your jungle of wine-bottle lamps,
Velvet pillows the color of blood pudding
And the white china flying fish from Italy.
I forget you, hearing the cut flowers
Sipping their liquids from assorted pots,
Pitchers and Coronation goblets
Like Monday drunkards. The milky berries
Bow down, a local constellation,
Toward their admirers in the tabletop:
Mobs of eyeballs looking up.
Are those petals of leaves you've paried with them ---
Those green-striped ovals of silver tissue?
The red geraniums I know.
Friends, friends. They stink of armpits
And the invovled maladies of autumn,
Musky as a lovebed the morning after.
My nostrils prickle with nostalgia.
Henna hags:cloth of your cloth.
They tow old water thick as fog.
The roses in the Toby jug
Gave up the ghost last night. High time.
Their yellow corsets were ready to split.
You snored, and I heard the petals unlatch,
Tapping and ticking like nervous fingers.
You should have junked them before they died.
Daybreak discovered the bureau lid
Littered with Chinese hands. Now I'm stared at
By chrysanthemums the size
Of Holofernes' head, dipped in the same
Magenta as this fubsy sofa.

In the mirror their doubles back them up.
Listen: your tenant mice
Are rattling the cracker packets. Fine flour
Muffles their bird feet: they whistle for joy.
And you doze on, nose to the wall.
This mizzle fits me like a sad jacket.
How did we make it up to your attic?
You handed me gin in a glass bud vase.
We slept like stones. Lady, what am I doing
With a lung full of dust and a tongue of wood,
Knee-deep in the cold swamped by flowers?
Submitted by Venus

Lesbos

Viciousness in the kitchen!
The potatoes hiss.
It is all Hollywood, windowless,
The fluorescent light wincing on and off like a terrible migraine,
Coy paper strips for doors --
Stage curtains, a widow's frizz.
And I, love, am a pathological liar,
And my child -- look at her, face down on the floor,
Little unstrung puppet, kicking to disappear --
Why she is schizophrenic,
Her face is red and white, a panic,
You have stuck her kittens outside your window
In a sort of cement well
Where they crap and puke and cry and she can't hear.
You say you can't stand her,
The bastard's a girl.
You who have blown your tubes like a bad radio
Clear of voices and history, the staticky
Noise of the new.
You say I should drown the kittens. Their smell!
You say I should drown my girl.
She'll cut her throat at ten if she's mad at two.
The baby smiles, fat snail,
From the polished lozenges of orange linoleum.
You could eat him. He's a boy.
You say your husband is just no good to you.
His Jew-Mama guards his sweet sex like a pearl.
You have one baby, I have two.
I should sit on a rock off Cornwall
and comb my hair.
I should wear tiger pants, I should have an affair.
We should meet in another life, we should meet in air,
Me and you.

Meanwhile there's a stink of fat and baby crap.
I'm doped and thick from my last sleeping pill.
The smog of cooking, the smog of hell
Floats our heads, two venemous opposites,
Our bones, our hair.
I call you Orphan, orphan. You are ill.
The sun gives you ulcers, the wind gives you T.B.
Once you were beautiful.
In New York, in Hollywood, the men said: 'Through?
Gee baby, you are rare.'
You acted, acted for the thrill.
The impotent husband slumps out for a coffee.
I try to keep him in,
An old pole for the lightning,
The acid baths, the skyfuls off of you.
He lumps it down the plastic cobbled hill,
Flogged trolley. The sparks are blue.
The blue sparks spill,
Splitting like quartz into a million bits.

O jewel! O valuable!
That night the moon
Dragged its blood bag, sick
Animal
Up over the harbor lights.
And then grew normal,
Hard and apart and white.
The scale-sheen on the sand scared me to death.
We kept picking up handfuls, loving it,
Working it like dough, a mulatto body,
The silk grits.
A dog picked up your doggy husband. He went on.
Now I am silent, hate
Up to my neck,
Thick, thick.
I do not speak.
I am packing the hard potatoes like good clothes,
I am packing the babies,

I am packing the sick cats.
O vase of acid,
It is love you are full of. You know who you hate.
He is hugging his ball and chain down by the gate
That opens to the sea
Where it drives in, white and black,
Then spews it back.
Every day you fill him with soul-stuff, like a pitcher.
You are so exhausted.
Your voice my ear-ring,
Flapping and sucking, blood-loving bat.
That is that. That is that.
You peer from the door,
Sad hag. 'Every woman's a whore.
I can't communicate.'
I see your cute décor
Close on you like the fist of a baby
Or an anemone, that sea
Sweetheart, that kleptomaniac.
I am still raw.
I say I may be back.
You know what lies are for.
Even in your Zen heaven we shan't meet.

Letter in November

Love, the world
Suddenly turns, turns color. The streetlight
Splits through the rat's tail
Pods of the laburnum at nine in the morning.
It is the Arctic,
This little black
Circle, with its tawn silk grasses - babies hair.
There is a green in the air,
Soft, delectable.
It cushions me lovingly.
I am flushed and warm.
I think I may be enormous,
I am so stupidly happy,
My Wellingtons
Squelching and squelching through the beautiful red.
This is my property.
Two times a day
I pace it, sniffing
The barbarous holly with its viridian
Scallops, pure iron,
And the wall of the odd corpses.
I love them.
I love them like history.
The apples are golden,
Imagine it . . .
My seventy trees
Holding their gold-ruddy balls
In a thick gray death-soup,
Their million
Gold leaves metal and breathless.
O love, O celibate.
Nobody but me
Walks the waist high wet.

The irreplaceable
Golds bleed and deepen, the mouths of Thermopylae.

Lorelei

It is no night to drown in:
A full moon, river lapsing
Black beneath bland mirror-sheen,
The blue water-mists dropping
Scrim after scrim like fishnets
Though fishermen are sleeping,
The massive castle turrets
Doubling themselves in a glass
All stillness. Yet these shapes float
Up toward me, troubling the face
Of quiet. From the nadir
They rise, their limbs ponderous
With richness, hair heavier
Than sculptured marble. They sing
Of a world more full and clear
Than can be. Sisters, your song
Bears a burden too weighty
For the whorled ear's listening
Here, in a well-steered country,
Under a balanced ruler.
Deranging by harmony
Beyond the mundane order,
Your voices lay siege. You lodge
On the pitched reefs of nightmare,
Promising sure harborage;
By day, descant from borders
Of hebetude, from the ledge
Also of high windows. Worse
Even than your maddening
Song, your silence. At the source
Of your ice-hearted calling --
Drunkenness of the great depths.
O river, I see drifting

Deep in your flux of silver
Those great goddesses of peace.
Stone, stone, ferry me down there.

Love Letter

Not easy to state the change you made.
If I'm alive now, then I was dead,
Though, like a stone, unbothered by it,
Staying put according to habit.
You didn't just tow me an inch, no-
Nor leave me to set my small bald eye
Skyward again, without hope, of course,
Of apprehending blueness, or stars.
That wasn't it. I slept, say: a snake
Masked among black rocks as a black rock
In the white hiatus of winter-
Like my neighbors, taking no pleasure
In the million perfectly-chisled
Cheeks alighting each moment to melt
My cheeks of basalt. They turned to tears,
Angels weeping over dull natures,
But didn't convince me. Those tears froze.
Each dead head had a visor of ice.
And I slept on like a bent finger.
The first thing I was was sheer air
And the locked drops rising in dew
Limpid as spirits. Many stones lay
Dense and expressionless round about.
I didn't know what to make of it.
I shone, mice-scaled, and unfolded
To pour myself out like a fluid
Among bird feet and the stems of plants.
I wasn't fooled. I knew you at once.
Tree and stone glittered, without shadows.
My finger-length grew lucent as glass.
I started to bud like a March twig:
An arm and a leg, and arm, a leg.
From stone to cloud, so I ascended.

Now I resemble a sort of god
Floating through the air in my soul-shift
Pure as a pane of ice. It's a gift.

Lyonnesse

No use whistling for Lyonnesse!
Sea-cold, sea-cold it certainly is.
Take a look at the white, high berg on his forehead-
There's where it sunk.
The blue, green,
Gray, indeterminate gilt
Sea of his eyes washing over it
And a round bubble
Popping upward from the mouths of bells
People and cows.
The Lyonians had always thought
Heaven would be something else,
But with the same faces,
The same places...
It was not a shock-
The clear, green, quite breathable atmosphere,
Cold grits underfoot,
And the spidery water-dazzle on field and street.
It never occurred that they had been forgot,
That the big God
Had lazily closed one eye and let them slip
Over the English cliff and under so much history!
They did not see him smile,
Turn, like an animal,
In his cage of ether, his cage of stars.
He'd had so many wars!
The white gape of his mind was the real Tabula Rasa.

Mad Girl's Love Song

"I shut my eyes and all the world drops dead;
I lift my lids and all is born again.
(I think I made you up inside my head.)
The stars go waltzing out in blue and red,
And arbitrary blackness gallops in:
I shut my eyes and all the world drops dead.
I dreamed that you bewitched me into bed
And sung me moon-struck, kissed me quite insane.
(I think I made you up inside my head.)
God topples from the sky, hell's fires fade:
Exit seraphim and Satan's men:
I shut my eyes and all the world drops dead.
I fancied you'd return the way you said,
But I grow old and I forget your name.
(I think I made you up inside my head.)
I should have loved a thunderbird instead;
At least when spring comes they roar back again.
I shut my eyes and all the world drops dead.
(I think I made you up inside my head.)"

Mary's Song

The Sunday lamb cracks in its fat.
The fat
Sacrifices its opacity. . . .
A window, holy gold.
The fire makes it precious,
The same fire
Melting the tallow heretics,
Ousting the Jews.
Their thick palls float
Over the cicatrix of Poland, burnt-out
Germany.
They do not die.
Grey birds obsess my heart,
Mouth-ash, ash of eye.
They settle. On the high
Precipice
That emptied one man into space
The ovens glowed like heavens, incandescent.
It is a heart,
This holocaust I walk in,
O golden child the world will kill and eat.

Medusa

Off that landspit of stony mouth-plugs,
Eyes rolled by white sticks,
Ears cupping the sea's incoherences,
You house your unnerving head--God-ball,
Lens of mercies,
Your stooges
Plying their wild cells in my keel's shadow,
Pushing by like hearts,
Red stigmata at the very center,
Riding the rip tide to the nearest point of
departure,
Dragging their Jesus hair.
Did I escape, I wonder?
My mind winds to you
Old barnacled umbilicus, Atlantic cable,
Keeping itself, it seems, in a state of miraculous
repair.
In any case, you are always there,
Tremulous breath at the end of my line,
Curve of water upleaping
To my water rod, dazzling and grateful,
Touching and sucking.
I didn't call you.
I didn't call you at all.
Nevertheless, nevertheless
You steamed to me over the sea,
Fat and red, a placenta
Paralyzing the kicking lovers.
Cobra light
Squeezing the breath from the blood bells
Of the fuchsia. I could draw no breath,
Dead and moneyless,
Overexposed, like an X-ray.

Who do you think you are?
A Communion wafer? Blubbery Mary?
I shall take no bite of your body,
Bottle in which I live,
Ghastly Vatican.
I am sick to death of hot salt.
Green as eunuchs, your wishes
Hiss at my sins.
Off, off, eely tentacle!
There is nothing between us.

Metaphors

I'm a riddle in nine syllables,
An elephant, a ponderous house,
A melon strolling on two tendrils.
O red fruit, ivory, fine timbers!
This loaf's big with its yeasty rising.
Money's new-minted in this fat purse.
I'm a means, a stage, a cow in calf.
I've eaten a bag of green apples,
Boarded the train there's no getting off.

Mirror

I am silver and exact. I have no preconceptions.
Whatever I see I swallow immediately
Just as it is, unmisted by love or dislike.
I am not cruel, only truthful ,
The eye of a little god, four-cornered.
Most of the time I meditate on the opposite wall.
It is pink, with speckles. I have looked at it so long
I think it is part of my heart. But it flickers.
Faces and darkness separate us over and over.
Now I am a lake. A woman bends over me,
Searching my reaches for what she really is.
Then she turns to those liars, the candles or the moon.
I see her back, and reflect it faithfully.
She rewards me with tears and an agitation of hands.
I am important to her. She comes and goes.
Each morning it is her face that replaces the darkness.
In me she has drowned a young girl, and in me an old woman
Rises toward her day after day, like a terrible fish.

Monologue At 3 AM

Better that every fiber crack
and fury make head,
blood drenching vivid
couch, carpet, floor
and the snake-figured almanac
vouching you are
a million green counties from here,
than to sit mute, twitching so
under prickling stars,
with stare, with curse
blackening the time
goodbyes were said, trains let go,
and I, great magnanimous fool, thus wrenched from
my one kingdom.
Submitted by Venus

Morning Song

Love set you going like a fat gold watch.
The midwife slapped your footsoles, and your bald cry
Took its place among the elements.
Our voices echo, magnifying your arrival. New statue.
In a drafty museum, your nakedness
Shadows our safety. We stand round blankly as walls.
I'm no more your mother
Than the cloud that distills a mirror to reflect its own slow
Effacement at the wind's hand.
All night your moth-breath
Flickers among the flat pink roses. I wake to listen:
A far sea moves in my ear.
One cry, and I stumble from bed, cow-heavy and floral
In my Victorian nightgown.
Your mouth opens clean as a cat's. The window square
Whitens and swallows its dull stars. And now you try
Your handful of notes;
The clear vowels rise like balloons.

Mushrooms

Overnight, very
Whitely, discreetly,
Very quietly
Our toes, our noses
Take hold on the loam,
Acquire the air.
Nobody sees us,
Stops us, betrays us;
The small grains make room.
Soft fists insist on
Heaving the needles,
The leafy bedding,
Even the paving.
Our hammers, our rams,
Earless and eyeless,
Perfectly voiceless,
Widen the crannies,
Shoulder through holes. We
Diet on water,
On crumbs of shadow,
Bland-mannered, asking
Little or nothing.
So many of us!
So many of us!
We are shelves, we are
Tables, we are meek,
We are edible,
Nudgers and shovers
In spite of ourselves.
Our kind multiplies:
We shall by morning
Inherit the earth.
Our foot's in the door.

Mystic

The air is a mill of hooks --
Questions without answer,
Glittering and drunk as flies
Whose kiss stings unbearably
In the fetid wombs of black air under pines in summer.
I remember
The dead smell of sun on wood cabins,
The stiffness of sails, the long salt winding sheets.
Once one has seen God, what is the remedy?
Once one has been seized up
Without a part left over,
Not a toe, not a finger, and used,
Used utterly, in the sun's conflagration, the stains
That lengthen from ancient cathedrals
What is the remedy?
The pill of the Communion tablet,
The walking beside still water? Memory?
Or picking up the bright pieces
Of Christ in the faces of rodents,
The tame flower-nibblers, the ones
Whose hopes are so low they are comfortable --
The humpback in his small, washed cottage
Under the spokes of the clematis.
Is there no great love, only tenderness?
Does the sea
Remember the walker upon it?
Meaning leaks from the molecules.
The chimneys of the city breathe, the window sweats,
The children leap in their cots.
The sun blooms, it is a geranium.
The heart has not stopped.

Never Try to Trick Me with a Kiss

Never try to trick me with a kiss
Pretending that the birds are here to stay;
The dying man will scoff and scorn at this.
A stone can masquerade where no heart is
And virgins rise where lustful Venus lay:
Never try to trick me with a kiss.
Our noble doctor claims the pain is his,
While stricken patients let him have his say;
The dying man will scoff and scorn at this.
Each virile bachelor dreads paralysis,
The old maid in the gable cries all day:
Never try to trick me with a kiss.
The suave eternal serpents promise bliss
To mortal children longing to be gay;
The dying man will scoff and scorn at this.
Sooner or later something goes amiss;
The singing birds pack up and fly away;
So never try to trick me with a kiss:
The dying man will scoff and scorn at this.

Nick and the Candlestick

I am a miner. The light burns blue.
Waxy stalactites
Drip and thicken, tears
The earthen womb
Exudes from its dead boredom.
Black bat airs
Wrap me, raggy shawls,
Cold homicides.
They weld to me like plums.
Old cave of calcium
Icicles, old echoer.
Even the newts are white,
Those holy Joes.
And the fish, the fish—
Christ! They are panes of ice,
A vice of knives,
A piranha
Religion, drinking
Its first communion out of my live toes.
The candle
Gulps and recovers its small altitude,
Its yellows hearten.
O love, how did you get here?
O embryo
Remembering, even in sleep,
Your crossed position.
The blood blooms clean
In you, ruby.
The pain
You wake to is not yours.
Love, love,
I have hung our cave with roses.
With soft rugs—

The last of Victoriana.
Let the stars
Plummet to their dark address,
Let the mercuric
Atoms that cripple drip
Into the terrible well,

You are the one
Solid the spaces lean on, envious.
You are the baby in the barn.

Night Shift

It was not a heart, beating.
That muted boom, that clangor
Far off, not blood in the ears
Drumming up and fever
To impose on the evening.
The noise came from outside:
A metal detonating
Native, evidently, to
These stilled suburbs nobody
Startled at it, though the sound
Shook the ground with its pounding.
It took a root at my coming
Till the thudding shource, exposed,
Counfounded in wept guesswork:
Framed in windows of Main Street's
Silver factory, immense
Hammers hoisted, wheels turning,
Stalled, let fall their vertical
Tonnage of metal and wood;
Stunned in marrow. Men in white
Undershirts circled, tending
Without stop those greased machines,
Tending, without stop, the blunt
Indefatigable fact.
Submitted by Venus

On Looking Into The Eyes Of A Demon Lover

Here are two pupils
whose moons of black
transform to cripples
all who look:
each lovely lady
who peers inside
take on the body
of a toad.
Within these mirrors
the world inverts:
the fond admirer's
burning darts
turn back to injure
the thrusting hand
and inflame to danger
the scarlet wound.
I sought my image
in the scorching glass,
for what fire could damage
a witch's face?
So I stared in that furnace
where beauties char
but found radiant Venus
reflected there.
Submitted by Venus

Paralytic

It happens. Will it go on? ----
My mind a rock,
No fingers to grip, no tongue,
My god the iron lung
That loves me, pumps
My two
Dust bags in and out,
Will not
Let me relapse
While the day outside glides by like ticker tape.
The night brings violets,
Tapestries of eyes,
Lights,
The soft anonymous
Talkers: 'You all right?'
The starched, inaccessible breast.
Dead egg, I lie
Whole
On a whole world I cannot touch,
At the white, tight
Drum of my sleeping couch
Photographs visit me-
My wife, dead and flat, in 1920 furs,
Mouth full of pearls,
Two girls
As flat as she, who whisper 'We're your daughters.'
The still waters
Wrap my lips,
Eyes, nose and ears,
A clear
Cellophane I cannot crack.
On my bare back
I smile, a buddha, all

Wants, desire
Falling from me like rings
Hugging their lights.
The claw
Of the magnolia,
Drunk on its own scents,
Asks nothing of life.

Perseus

The Triumph of Wit Over Suffering
Head alone shows you in the prodigious act
Of digesting what centuries alone digest:
The mammoth, lumbering statuary of sorrow,
Indissoluble enough to riddle the guts
Of a whale with holes and holes, and bleed him white
Into salt seas. Hercules had a simple time,
Rinsing those stables: a baby's tears would do it.
But who'd volunteer to gulp the Laocoon,
The Dying Gaul and those innumerable pietas
Festering on the dim walls of Europe's chapels,
Museums and sepulchers? You.
You
Who borrowed feathers for your feet, not lead,
Not nails, and a mirror to keep the snaky head
In safe perspective, could outface the gorgon-grimace
Of human agony: a look to numb
Limbs: not a basilisk-blink, nor a double whammy,
But all the accumulated last grunts, groans,
Cries and heroic couplets concluding the million
Enacted tragedies on these blood-soaked boards,
And every private twinge a hissing asp
To petrify your eyes, and every village
Catastrophe a writhing length of cobra,
And the decline of empires the thick coil of a vast
Anacnoda.
Imagine: the world
Fisted to a foetus head, ravined, seamed
With suffering from conception upwards, and there
You have it in hand. Grit in the eye or a sore
Thumb can make anyone wince, but the whole globe
Expressive of grief turns gods, like kings, to rocks.
Those rocks, cleft and worn, themselves then grow

Ponderous and extend despair on earth's
Dark face.
So might rigor mortis come to stiffen
All creation, were it not for a bigger belly
Still than swallows joy.
You enter now,
Armed with feathers to tickle as well as fly,
And a fun-house mirror that turns the tragic muse
To the beheaded head of a sullen doll, one braid,
A bedraggled snake, hanging limp as the absurd mouth
Hangs in its lugubious pout. Where are
The classic limbs of stubborn Antigone?
The red, royal robes of Phedre? The tear-dazzled
Sorrows of Malfi's gentle duchess?
Gone
In the deep convulsion gripping your face, muscles
And sinews bunched, victorious, as the cosmic
Laugh does away with the unstitching, plaguey wounds

Of an eternal sufferer.
To you
Perseus, the palm, and may you poise
And repoise until time stop, the celestial balance
Which weighs our madness with our sanity.

Poems, Potatoes

The word, defining, muzzles; the drawn line
Ousts mistier peers and thrives, murderous,
In establishments which imagined lines
Can only haunt. Sturdy as potatoes,
Stones, without conscience, word and line endure,
Given an inch. Not that they're gross (although
Afterthought often would have them alter
To delicacy, to poise) but that they
Shortchange me continuously: whether
More or other, they still dissatisfy.
Unpoemed, unpictured, the potato
Bunches its knobby browns on a vastly
Superior page; the blunt stone also.

Polly's Tree

A dream tree, Polly's tree:
a thicket of sticks,
each speckled twig
ending in a thin-paned
leaf unlike any
other on it
or in a ghost flower
flat as paper and
of a color
vaporish as frost-breath,
more finical than
any silk fan
the Chinese ladies use
to stir robin's egg
air. The silver -
haired seed of the milkweed
comes to roost there, frail
as the halo
rayed round a candle flame,
a will-o'-the-wisp
nimbus, or puff
of cloud-stuff, tipping her
queer candelabrum.
Palely lit by
snuff-ruffed dandelions,
white daisy wheels and
a tiger faced
pansy, it glows. O it's
no family tree,
Polly's tree, nor
a tree of heaven, though
it marry quartz-flake,
feather and rose.

It sprang from her pillow
whole as a cobweb
ribbed like a hand,
a dream tree. Polly's tree
wears a valentine
arc of tear-pearled
bleeding hearts on its sleeve
and, crowning it, one
blue larkspur star.

Poppies In July

Little poppies, little hell flames,
Do you do no harm?
You flicker. I cannot touch you.
I put my hands among the flames. Nothing burns
And it exhausts me to watch you
Flickering like that, wrinkly and clear red, like the skin of a mouth.
A mouth just bloodied.
Little bloody skirts!
There are fumes I cannot touch.
Where are your opiates, your nauseous capsules?
If I could bleed, or sleep! -
If my mouth could marry a hurt like that!
Or your liquors seep to me, in this glass capsule,
Dulling and stilling.
But colorless. Colorless.

Poppies in October

Even the sun-clouds this morning cannot manage such skirts.
Nor the woman in the ambulance
Whose red heart blooms through her coat so astoundingly --
A gift, a love gift
Utterly unasked for
By a sky
Palely and flamily
Igniting its carbon monoxides, by eyes
Dulled to a halt under bowlers.
O my God, what am I
That these late mouths should cry open
In a forest of frost, in a dawn of cornflowers.

Prospect

Among orange-tile rooftops
and chimney pots
the fen fog slips,
gray as rats,
while on spotted branch
of the sycamore
two black rooks hunch
and darkly glare,
watching for night,
with absinthe eye
cocked on the lone, late,
passer-by.

Purdah

Jade --
Stone of the side,
The antagonized
Side of green Adam, I
Smile, cross-legged,
Enigmatical,
Shifting my clarities.
So valuable!
How the sun polishes this shoulder!
And should
The moon, my
Indefatigable cousin
Rise, with her cancerous pallors,
Dragging trees --
Little bushy polyps,
Little nets,
My visibilities hide.
I gleam like a mirror.
At this facet the bridegroom arrives
Lord of the mirrors!
It is himself he guides
In among these silk
Screens, these rustling appurtenances.
I breathe, and the mouth
Veil stirs its curtain
My eye
Veil is
A concatenation of rainbows.
I am his.
Even in his
Absence, I
Revolve in my
Sheath of impossibles,

Priceless and quiet
Among these parrakeets, macaws!
O chatterers
Attendants of the eyelash!
I shall unloose
One feather, like the peacock.

Attendants of the lip!
I shall unloose
One note
Shattering
The chandelier
Of air that all day flies
Its crystals
A million ignorants.
Attendants!
Attendants!
And at his next step
I shall unloose
I shall unloose --
From the small jeweled
Doll he guards like a heart --
The lioness,
The shriek in the bath,
The cloak of holes.

Pursuit

There is a panther stalks me down:
One day I'll have my death of him;
His greed has set the woods aflame,
He prowls more lordly than the sun.
Most soft, most suavely glides that step,
Advancing always at my back;
From gaunt hemlock, rooks croak havoc:
The hunt is on, and sprung the trap.
Flayed by thorns I trek the rocks,
Haggard through the hot white noon.
Along red network of his veins
What fires run, what craving wakes?

Insatiate, he ransacks the land
Condemned by our ancestral fault,
Crying: blood, let blood be spilt;
Meat must glut his mouth's raw wound.
Keen the rending teeth and sweet
The singeing fury of his fur;
His kisses parch, each paw's a briar,
Doom consummates that appetite.
In the wake of this fierce cat,
Kindled like torches for his joy,
Charred and ravened women lie,
Become his starving body's bait.

Now hills hatch menace, spawning shade;
Midnight cloaks the sultry grove;
The black marauder, hauled by love
On fluent haunches, keeps my speed.
Behind snarled thickets of my eyes
Lurks the lithe one; in dreams' ambush
Bright those claws that mar the flesh

And hungry, hungry, those taut thighs.
His ardor snares me, lights the trees,
And I run flaring in my skin;
What lull, what cool can lap me in
When burns and brands that yellow gaze?
I hurl my heart to halt his pace,
To quench his thirst I squander blood;
He eats, and still his need seeks food,
Compels a total sacrifice.
His voice waylays me, spells a trance,
The gutted forest falls to ash;
Appalled by secret want, I rush
From such assault of radiance.
Entering the tower of my fears,

I shut my doors on that dark guilt,
I bolt the door, each door I bolt.
Blood quickens, gonging in my ears:
The panther's tread is on the stairs,
Coming up and up the stairs.

Resolve

Day of mist: day of tarnish
with hands
unserviceable, I wait
for the milk van
the one-eared cat
laps its gray paw
and the coal fire burns
outside, the little hedge leaves are
become quite yellow
a milk-film blurs
the empty bottles on the windowsill
no glory descends
two water drops poise
on the arched green
stem of my neighbor's rose bush
o bent bow of thorns
the cat unsheathes its claws
the world turns
today
today I will not
disenchant my twelve black-gowned examiners
or bunch my fist
in the wind's sneer.

Sculptor

To his house the bodiless
Come to barter endlessly
Vision, wisdom, for bodies
Palpable as his, and weighty.
Hands moving move priestlier
Than priest's hands, invoke no vain
Images of light and air
But sure stations in bronze, wood, stone.
Obdurate, in dense-grained wood,
A bald angel blocks and shapes
The flimsy light; arms folded
Watches his cumbrous world eclipse
Inane worlds of wind and cloud.
Bronze dead dominate the floor,
Resistive, ruddy-bodied,
Dwarfing us. Our bodies flicker
Toward extinction in those eyes
Which, without him, were beggared
Of place, time, and their bodies.
Emulous spirits make discord,
Try entry, enter nightmares
Until his chisel bequeaths
Them life livelier than ours,
A solider repose than death's.

Sheep in Fog

The hills step off into whiteness.
People or stars
Regard me sadly, I disappoint them.
The train leaves a line of breath.
O slow
Horse the colour of rust,
Hooves, dolorous bells -
All morning the
Morning has been blackening,
A flower left out.
My bones hold a stillness, the far
Fields melt my heart.
They threaten
To let me through to a heaven
Starless and fatherless, a dark water.

Sleep in the Mojave Desert

Out here there are no hearthstones,
Hot grains, simply. It is dry, dry.
And the air dangerous. Noonday acts queerly
On the mind's eye erecting a line
Of poplars in the middle distance, the only
Object beside the mad, straight road
One can remember men and houses by.
A cool wind should inhabit these leaves
And a dew collect on them, dearer than money,
In the blue hour before sunup.
Yet they recede, untouchable as tomorrow,
Or those glittery fictions of spilt water
That glide ahead of the very thirsty.
I think of the lizards airing their tongues
In the crevice of an extremely small shadow
And the toad guarding his heart's droplet.
The desert is white as a blind man's eye,
Comfortless as salt. Snake and bird
Doze behind the old maskss of fury.
We swelter like firedogs in the wind.
The sun puts its cinder out. Where we lie
The heat-cracked crickets congregate
In their black armorplate and cry.
The day-moon lights up like a sorry mother,
And the crickets come creeping into our hair
To fiddle the short night away.

Sleepers

No map traces the street
Where those two sleepers are.
We have lost track of it.
They lie as if under water
In a blue, unchanging light,
The French window ajar
Curtained with yellow lace.
Through the narrow crack
Odors of wet earth rise.
The snail leaves a silver track;
Dark thickets hedge the house.
We take a backward look.
Among petals pale as death
And leaves steadfast in shape
They sleep on, mouth to mouth.
A white mist is going up.
The small green nostrils breathe,
And they turn in their sleep.
Ousted from that warm bed
We are a dream they dream.
Their eyelids keep up the shade.
No harm can come to them.
We cast our skins and slide
Into another time.

Snakecharmer

As the gods began one world, and man another,
So the snakecharmer begins a snaky sphere
With moon-eye, mouth-pipe, He pipes. Pipes green. Pipes water.
Pipes water green until green waters waver
With reedy lengths and necks and undulatings.
And as his notes twine green, the green river
Shapes its images around his sons.
He pipes a place to stand on, but no rocks,
No floor: a wave of flickering grass tongues
Supports his foot. He pipes a world of snakes,
Of sways and coilings, from the snake-rooted bottom
Of his mind. And now nothing but snakes
Is visible. The snake-scales have become
Leaf, become eyelid; snake-bodies, bough, breast
Of tree and human. And he within this snakedom
Rules the writhings which make manifest
His snakehood and his might with pliant tunes
From his thin pipe. Out of this green nest
As out of Eden's navel twist the lines
Of snaky generations: let there be snakes!
And snakes there were, are, will be--till yawns
Consume this pipe and he tires of music
And pipes the world back to the simple fabric
Of snake-warp, snake-weft. Pipes the cloth of snakes
To a melting of green waters, till no snake
Shows its head, and those green waters back to
Water, to green, to nothing like a snake.
Puts up his pipe, and lids his moony eye.

Southern Sunrise

Color of lemon, mango, peach,
These storybook villas
Still dream behind
Shutters, thier balconies
Fine as hand-
Made lace, or a leaf-and-flower pen-sketch.
Tilting with the winds,
On arrowy stems,
Pineapple-barked,
A green crescent of palms
Sends up its forked
Firework of fronds.
A quartz-clear dawn
Inch by bright inch
Gilds all our Avenue,
And out of the blue drench
Of Angels' Bay
Rises the round red watermelon sun.

Sow

God knows how our neighbor managed to breed
  His great sow:
Whatever his shrewd secret, he kept it hid
  In the same way
He kept the sow--impounded from public stare,
  Prize ribbon and pig show.

But one dusk our questions commended us to a tour
  Through his lantern-lit
Maze of barns to the lintel of the sunk sty door
  To gape at it:
This was no rose-and-larkspurred china suckling
  With a penny slot

For thrift children, nor dolt pig ripe for heckling,
  About to be
Glorified for prime flesh and golden crackling
  In a parsley halo;
Nor even one of the common barnyard sows,
  Mire-smirched, blowzy,

Maunching thistle and knotweed on her snoutcruise--
  Bloat tun of milk
On the move, hedged by a litter of feat-foot ninnies
  Shrilling her hulk
To halt for a swig at the pink teats. No. This vast
  Brobdingnag bulk

Of a sow lounged belly-bedded on that black
  compost,
  Fat-rutted eyes
  Dream-filmed.
What a vision of ancient hoghood must
  Thus wholly engross
The great grandam!--our marvel blazoned a knight,
  Helmed, in cuirass,
Unhorsed and shredded in the grove of combat

By a grisly-bristled
Boar, fabulous enough to straddle that sow's heat.
But our farmer whistled,
Then, with a jocular fist thwacked the barrel nape,
And the green-copse-castled
Pig hove, letting legend like dried mud drop,

Slowly, grunt
On grunt, up in the flickering light to shape
A monument
Prodigious in gluttonies as that hog whose want
Made lean Lent
Of kitchen slops and, stomaching no constraint,
Proceeded to swill
The seven troughed seas and every earthquaking
continent.

Spinster

Now this particular girl
During a ceremonious april walk
With her latest suitor
Found herself, of a sudden, intolerably struck
By the bird's irregular babel
And the leaves' litter.

By this tumult afflicted, she
Observed her lover's gestures unbalance the air,
His gait stray uneven
Through a rank wilderness of fern and flower;
She judged petals in disarray,
The whole season, sloven.

How she longed for winter then!-
Scrupulously austere in its order
Of white and black
Ice and rock; each sentiment within border,
And heart's frosty discipline
Exact as a snowflake.

But here - a burgeoning
Unruly enough to pitch her five queenly wits
Into vulgar motley-
A treason not to be borne; let idiots
Reel giddy in bedlam spring;
She withdrew neatly.

And round her house she set
Such a barricade of barb and check
Against mutinous weather
As no mere insurgent man could hope to break
With curse, fist, threat
Or love, either.

Stillborn

These poems do not live: it's a sad diagnosis.
They grew their toes and fingers well enough,
Their little foreheads bulged with concentration.
If they missed out on walking about like people
It wasn't for any lack of mother-love.
O I cannot explain what happened to them!
They are proper in shape and number and every part.
They sit so nicely in the pickling fluid!
They smile and smile and smile at me.
And still the lungs won't fill and the heart won't start.
They are not pigs, they are not even fish,
Though they have a piggy and a fishy air --
It would be better if they were alive, and that's what they were.
But they are dead, and their mother near dead with distraction,
And they stupidly stare and do not speak of her.

Bare-handed, I hand the combs.

The man in white smiles, bare-handed,
Our cheesecloth gauntlets neat and sweet,
The throats of our wrists brave lilies.
He and I
Have a thousand clean cells between us,
Eight combs of yellow cups,
And the hive itself a teacup,
White with pink flowers on it,
With excessive love I enameled it
Thinking 'Sweetness, sweetness.'
Brood cells gray as the fossils of shells
Terrify me, they seem so old.
What am I buying, wormy mahogany?
Is there any queen at all in it?
If there is, she is old,
Her wings torn shawls, her long body
Rubbed of its plush ----
Poor and bare and unqueenly and even shameful.
I stand in a column
Of winged, unmiraculous women,
Honey-drudgers.
I am no drudge
Though for years I have eaten dust
And dried plates with my dense hair.
And seen my strangeness evaporate,
Blue dew from dangerous skin.
Will they hate me,
These women who only scurry,
Whose news is the open cherry, the open clover?
It is almost over.
I am in control.
Here is my honey-machine,
It will work without thinking,

Opening, in spring, like an industrious virgin
To scour the creaming crests
As the moon, for its ivory powders, scours the sea.
A third person is watching.
He has nothing to do with the bee-seller or with me.
Now he is gone
In eight great bounds, a great scapegoat.
Here is his slipper, here is another,
And here the square of white linen
He wore instead of a hat.

He was sweet,

The sweat of his efforts a rain
Tugging the world to fruit.
The bees found him out,
Molding onto his lips like lies,
Complicating his features.
They thought death was worth it, but I
Have a self to recover, a queen.
Is she dead, is she sleeping?
Where has she been,
With her lion-red body, her wings of glass?
Now she is flying
More terrible than she ever was, red
Scar in the sky, red comet
Over the engine that killed her ----
The mausoleum, the wax house.

Strumpet Song

With white frost gone
And all green dreams not worth much,
After a lean day's work
Time comes round for that foul slut:
Mere bruit of her takes our street
Until every man,
Red, pale or dark,
Veers to her slouch.
Mark, I cry, that mouth
Made to do violence on,
That seamed face
Askew with blotch, dint, scar
Struck by each dour year.
Walks there not some such one man
As can spare breath
To patch with brand of love this rank grimace
Which out from black tarn, ditch and cup
Into my most chaste own eyes
Looks up.

Tale of a Tub

The photographic chamber of the eye
records bare painted walls, while an electric light
lays the chromium nerves of plumbing raw;
such poverty assaults the ego; caught
naked in the merely actual room,
the stranger in the lavatory mirror
puts on a public grin, repeats our name
but scrupulously reflects the usual terror.
Just how guilty are we when the ceiling
reveals no cracks that can be decoded? when washbowl
maintains it has no more holy calling
than physical ablution, and the towel
dryly disclaims that fierce troll faces lurk
in its explicit folds? or when the window,
blind with steam, will not admit the dark
which shrouds our prospects in ambiguous shadow?
Twenty years ago, the familiar tub
bred an ample batch of omens; but now
water faucets spawn no danger; each crab
and octopus -- scrabbling just beyond the view,
waiting for some accidental break
in ritual, to strike -- is definitely gone;
the authentic sea denies them and will pluck
fantastic flesh down to the honest bone.
We take the plunge; under water our limbs
waver, faintly green, shuddering away
from the genuine color of skin; can our dreams
ever blur the intransigent lines which draw
the shape that shuts us in? absolute fact
intrudes even when the revolted eye
is closed; the tub exists behind our back;
its glittering surfaces are blank and true.
Yet always the ridiculous nude flanks urge

the fabrication of some cloth to cover
such starkness; accuracy must not stalk at large:
each day demands we create our whole world over,
disguising the constant horror in a coat
of many-colored fictions; we mask our past
in the green of Eden, pretend future's shining fruit
can sprout from the navel of this present waste.
In this particular tub, two knees jut up
like icebergs, while minute brown hairs rise
on arms and legs in a fringe of kelp; green soap
navigates the tidal slosh of seas
breaking on legendary beaches; in faith
we shall board our imagined ship and wildly sail
among sacred islands of the mad till death
shatters the fabulous stars and makes us real.

The Applicant

First, are you our sort of a person?
Do you wear
A glass eye, false teeth or a crutch,
A brace or a hook,
Rubber breasts or a rubber crotch,
Stitches to show something's missing? No, no? Then
How can we give you a thing?
Stop crying.
Open your hand.
Empty? Empty. Here is a hand
To fill it and willing
To bring teacups and roll away headaches
And do whatever you tell it.
Will you marry it?
It is guaranteed
To thumb shut your eyes at the end
And dissolve of sorrow.
We make new stock from the salt.
I notice you are stark naked.
How about this suit----
Black and stiff, but not a bad fit.
Will you marry it?
It is waterproof, shatterproof, proof
Against fire and bombs through the roof.
Believe me, they'll bury you in it.
Now your head, excuse me, is empty.
I have the ticket for that.
Come here, sweetie, out of the closet.
Well, what do you think of that ?
Naked as paper to start
But in twenty-five years she'll be silver,
In fifty, gold.
A living doll, everywhere you look.

It can sew, it can cook,
It can talk, talk , talk.
It works, there is nothing wrong with it.
You have a hole, it's a poultice.
You have an eye, it's an image.
My boy, it's your last resort.
Will you marry it, marry it, marry it.

The Arrival of the Bee Box

I ordered this, clean wood box
Square as a chair and almost too heavy to lift.
I would say it was the coffin of a midget
Or a square baby
Were there not such a din in it.

The box is locked, it is dangerous.
I have to live with it overnight
And I can't keep away from it.
There are no windows, so I can't see what is in there.
There is only a little grid, no exit.

I put my eye to the grid.
It is dark, dark,
With the swarmy feeling of African hands
Minute and shrunk for export,
Black on black, angrily clambering.

How can I let them out?
It is the noise that appalls me most of all,
The unintelligible syllables.
It is like a Roman mob,
Small, taken one by one, but my god, together!

I lay my ear to furious Latin.
I am not a Caesar.
I have simply ordered a box of maniacs.
They can be sent back.
They can die, I need feed them nothing, I am the owner.

I wonder how hungry they are.
I wonder if they would forget me
If I just undid the locks and s
tood back and turned into a tree.
There is the laburnum, its blond colonnades,

And the petticoats of the cherry.
They might ignore me immediately
In my moon suit and funeral veil.

I am no source of honey
So why should they turn on me?
Tomorrow I will be sweet God, I will set them free.
The box is only temporary.

The Bee Meeting

Who are these people at the bridge to meet me? They are the
villagers----
The rector, the midwife, the sexton, the agent for bees.
In my sleeveless summery dress I have no protection,
And they are all gloved and covered, why did nobody tell me?
They are smiling and taking out veils tacked to ancient hats.
I am nude as a chicken neck, does nobody love me?
Yes, here is the secretary of bees with her white shop smock,
Buttoning the cuffs at my wrists and the slit from my neck to my
knees.
Now I am milkweed silk, the bees will not notice.
They will not smell my fear, my fear, my fear.
Which is the rector now, is it that man in black?
Which is the midwife, is that her blue coat?
Everybody is nodding a square black head, they are knights in visors,
Breastplates of cheesecloth knotted under the armpits.
Their smiles and their voces are changing. I am led through a
beanfield.
Strips of tinfoil winking like people,
Feather dusters fanning their hands in a sea of bean flowers,
Creamy bean flowers with black eyes and leaves like bored hearts.
Is it blood clots the tendrils are dragging up that string?
No, no, it is scarlet flowers that will one day be edible.
Now they are giving me a fashionable white straw Italian hat
And a black veil that molds to my face,
they are making me one of them.
They are leading me to the shorn grove,
the circle of hives.
Is it the hawthorn that smells so sick?
The barren body of hawthon, etherizing
its children.
Is it some operation that is taking place?
It is the surgeon my neighbors are waiting for,

This apparition in a green helmet,
Shining gloves and white suit.
Is it the butcher, the grocer, the postman, someone I know?
I cannot run, I am rooted, and the gorse hurts me
With its yellow purses, its spiky armory.
I could not run without having to run forever.
The white hive is snug as a virgin,
Sealing off her brood cells, her honey, and quietly humming.
Smoke rolls and scarves in the grove.
The mind of the hive thinks this is the end of everything.
Here they come, the outriders, on their hysterical elastics.
If I stand very still, they will think I am cow-parsley,
A gullible head untouched by their animosity,
Not even nodding, a personage in a hedgerow.
The villagers open the chambers, they are hunting the queen.
Is she hiding, is she eating honey? She is very clever.
She is old, old, old, she must live another year, and she knows it.

While in their fingerjoint cells the new virgins
Dream of a duel they will win inevitably,
A curtain of wax dividing them from the bride flight,
The upflight of the murderess into a heaven that loves her.
The villagers are moving the virgins, there will be no killing.
The old queen does not show herself, is she so ungrateful?
I am exhausted, I am exhausted ----
Pillar of white in a blackout of knives.
I am the magician's girl who does not flinch.
The villagers are untying their disguises, they are shaking hands.
Whose is that long white box in the grove, what have they
accomplished, why am I cold.

The Bull of Bendylaw

The black bull bellowed before the sea.
The sea, till that day orderly,
Hove up against Bendylaw.
The queen in the mulberry arbor stared
Stiff as a queen on a playing card.
The king fingered his beard.
A blue sea, four horny bull-feet,
A bull-snouted sea that wouldn't stay put,
Bucked at the garden gate.
Along box-lined walks in the florid sun
Toward the rowdy bellow and back again
The lords and ladies ran.
The great bronze gate began to crack,
The sea broke in at every crack,
Pellmell, blueblack.
The bull surged up, the bull surged down,
Not to be stayed by a daisy chain
Nor by any learned man.
O the king's tidy acre is under the sea,
And the royal rose in the bull's belly,
And the bull on the king's highway.

The Colossus

I shall never get you put together entirely,
Pieced, glued, and properly jointed.
Mule-bray, pig-grunt and bawdy cackles
Proceed from your great lips.
It's worse than a barnyard.

Perhaps you consider yourself an oracle,
Mouthpiece of the dead, or of some god or other.
Thirty years now I have labored
To dredge the silt from your throat.
I am none the wiser.

Scaling little ladders with glue pots and pails of Lysol
I crawl like an ant in mourning
Over the weedy acres of your brow
To mend the immense skull-plates and clear
The bald, white tumuli of your eyes.

A blue sky out of the Oresteia
Arches above us. O father, all by yourself
You are pithy and historical as the Roman Forum.
I open my lunch on a hill of black cypress.
Your fluted bones and acanthine hair are littered

In their old anarchy to the horizon-line.
It would take more than a lightning-stroke
To create such a ruin.
Nights, I squat in the cornucopia
Of your left ear, out of the wind,

Counting the red stars and those of plum-color.
The sun rises under the pillar of your tongue.
My hours are married to shadow.
No longer do I listen for the scrape of a keel
On the blank stones of the landing.

The Couriers

The word of a snail on the plate of a leaf?
It is not mine. Do not accept it.
Acetic acid in a sealed tin?
Do not accept it. It is not genuine.
A ring of gold with the sun in it?
Lies. Lies and a grief.
Frost on a leaf, the immaculate
Cauldron, talking and crackling
All to itself on the top of each
Of nine black Alps.
A disturbance in mirrors,
The sea shattering its grey one ----
Love, love, my season.

The Dead

Revolving in oval loops of solar speed,
Couched in cauls of clay as in holy robes,
Dead men render love and war no heed,
Lulled in the ample womb of the full-tilt globe.
No spiritual Caesars are these dead;
They want no proud paternal kingdom come;
And when at last they blunder into bed
World-wrecked, they seek only oblivion.
Rolled round with goodly loam and cradled deep,
These bone shanks will not wake immaculate
To trumpet-toppling dawn of doomstruck day :
They loll forever in colossal sleep;
Nor can God's stern, shocked angels cry them up
From their fond, final, infamous decay.
Anonymous submission.

The Disquieting Muses

Mother, mother, what ill-bred aunt
Or what disfigured and unsightly
Cousin did you so unwisely keep
Unasked to my christening, that she
Sent these ladies in her stead
With heads like darning-eggs to nod
And nod and nod at foot and head
And at the left side of my crib?
Mother, who made to order stories
Of Mixie Blackshort the heroic bear,
Mother, whose witches always, always
Got baked into gingerbread, I wonder
Whether you saw them, whether you said
Words to rid me of those three ladies
Nodding by night around my bed,
Mouthless, eyeless, with stitched bald head.
In the hurricane, when father's twelve
Study windows bellied in
Like bubbles about to break, you fed
My brother and me cookies and Ovaltine
And helped the two of us to choir:
'Thor is angry; boom boom boom!
Thor is angry: we don't care!'
But those ladies broke the panes.
When on tiptoe the schoolgirls danced,
Blinking flashlights like fireflies
And singing the glowworm song, I could
Not lift a foot in the twinkle-dress
But, heavy-footed, stood aside
In the shadow cast by my dismal-headed
Godmothers, and you cried and cried:
And the shadow stretched, the lights went out.
Mother, you sent me to piano lessons

And praised my arabesques and trills
Although each teacher found my touch
Oddly wooden in spite of scales
And the hours of practicing, my ear
Tone-deaf and yes, unteachable.
I learned, I learned, I learned elsewhere,
From muses unhired by you, dear mother.
I woke one day to see you, mother,
Floating above me in bluest air
On a green balloon bright with a million
Flowers and bluebirds that never were
Never, never, found anywhere.
But the little planet bobbed away
Like a soap-bubble as you called: Come here!

And I faced my traveling companions.
Day now, night now, at head, side, feet,
They stand their vigil in gowns of stone,
Faces blank as the day I was born.
Their shadows long in the setting sun
That never brightens or goes down.
And this is the kingdom you bore me to,
Mother, mother. But no frown of mine
Will betray the company I keep.

The Eye-Mote

Blameless as daylight I stood looking
At a field of horses, necks bent, manes blown,
Tails streaming against the green
Backdrop of sycamores. Sun was striking
White chapel pinnacles over the roofs,
Holding the horses, the clouds, the leaves
Steadily rooted though they were all flowing
Away to the left like reeds in a sea
When the splinter flew in and stuck my eye,
Needling it dark. Then I was seeing
A melding of shapes in a hot rain:
Horses warped on the altering green,
Outlandish as double-humped camels or unicorns,
Grazing at the margins of a bad monochrome,
Beasts of oasis, a better time.
Abrading my lid, the small grain burns:
Red cinder around which I myself,
Horses, planets and spires revolve.
Neither tears nor the easing flush
Of eyebaths can unseat the speck:
It sticks, and it has stuck a week.
I wear the present itch for flesh,
Blind to what will be and what was.
I dream that I am Oedipus.
What I want back is what I was
Before the bed, before the knife,
Before the brooch-pin and the salve
Fixed me in this parenthesis;
Horses fluent in the wind,
A place, a time gone out of mind.

The Moon and the Yew tree

"This is the light of the mind, cold and planetary.
The trees of the mind are black. The light is blue.
The grasses unload their griefs at my feet as if I were God,
Prickling my ankles and murmuring of their humility.
Fumy spiritious mists inhabit this place
Separated from my house by a row of headstones.
I simply cannot see where there is to get to.
The moon is no door. It is a face in its own right,
White as a knuckle and terribly upset.
It drags the sea after it like a dark crime; it is quiet
With the O-gape of complete despair. I live here.
Twice on Sunday, the bells startle the sky -
Eight great tongues affirming the Resurrection.
At the end, they soberly bong out their names.
The yew tree points up. It has a Gothic shape.
The eyes lift after it and find the moon.
The moon is my mother. She is not sweet like Mary.
Her blue garments unloose small bats and owls.
How I would like to believe in tenderness -
The face of the effigy, gentled by candles,
Bending, on me in particular, its mild eyes.
I have fallen a long way. Clouds are flowering
Blue and mystical over the face of the stars.
Inside the church, the saints will be all blue,
Floating on their delicate feet over cold pews,
Their hands and faces stiff with holiness.
The moon sees nothing of this. She is bald and wild.
And the message of the yew tree is blackness - blackness a
silence."

The Munich Mannequins

Perfection is terrible, it cannot have children.
Cold as snow breath, it tamps the womb
Where the yew trees blow like hydras,
The tree of life and the tree of life
Unloosing their moons, month after month, to no purpose.
The blood flood is the flood of love,
The absolute sacrifice.
It means: no more idols but me,
Me and you.
So, in their sulfur loveliness, in their smiles
These mannequins lean tonight
In Munich, morgue between Paris and Rome,
Naked and bald in their furs,
Orange lollies on silver sticks,
Intolerable, without mind.
The snow drops its pieces of darkness,
Nobody's about. In the hotels
Hands will be opening doors and setting
Down shoes for a polish of carbon
Into which broad toes will go tomorrow.
O the domesticity of these windows,
The baby lace, the green-leaved confectionery,
The thick Germans slumbering in their bottomless Stolz.
And the black phones on hooks
Glittering
Glittering and digesting
Voicelessness. The snow has no voice.
28 January 1963

The Night Dances

A smile fell in the grass. Irretrievable!
And how will your night dances Lose themselves. In mathematics?
Such pure leaps and spirals ----
Surely they travel
The world forever, I shall not entirely Sit emptied of beauties, the gift
Of your small breath, the drenched grass Smell of your sleeps, lilies,
lilies.
Their flesh bears no relation. Cold folds of ego, the calla,
And the tiger, embellishing itself ----
Spots, and a spread of hot petals.
The comets
Have such a space to cross,
Such coldness, forgetfulness. So your gestures flake off ----
Warm and human, then their pink light Bleeding and peeling
Through the black amnesias of heaven. Why am I given
These lamps, these planets Falling like blessings, like flakes
Six sided, white
On my eyes, my lips, my hair
Touching and melting. Nowhere.

The Other

You come in late, wiping your lips.
What did I leave untouched on the doorstep---
White Nike,
Streaming between my walls?
Smilingly, blue lightning
Assumes, like a meathook, the burden of his parts.
The police love you, you confess everything. Bright hair, shoe-black,
old plastic,
Is my life so intriguing?
Is it for this you widen your eye-rings?
Is it for this the air motes depart?
They rae not air motes, they are corpuscles.
Open your handbag. What is that bad smell? It is your knitting, busily
Hooking itself to itself, It is your sticky candies.
I have your head on my wall. Navel cords, blue-red and lucent,
Shriek from my belly like arrows, and these I ride. O moon-glow, o
sick one,
The stolen horses, the fornications Circle a womb of marble.
Where are you going
That you suck breath like mileage?
Sulfurous adulteries grieve in a dream. Cold glass, how you insert
yourself
Between myself and myself. I scratch like a cat.
The blood that runs is dark fruit--- An effect, a cosmetic.
You smile.
No, it is not fatal.

Submitted by Venus

The Other Two

All summer we moved in a villa brimful of echos,
Cool as the pearled interior of a conch.
Bells, hooves, of the high-stipping black goats woke us.
Around our bed the baronial furniture
Foundered through levels of light seagreen and strange.
Not one leaf wrinkled in the clearing air.
We dreamed how we were perfect, and we were.
Against bare, whitewashed walls, the furniture Anchored itself,
griffin-legged and darkly grained.
Two of us in a place meant for ten more-
Our footsteps multiplied in the shadowy chambers,
Our voices fathomed a profounder sound:
The walnut banquet table, the twelve chairs
Mirrored the intricate gestures of two others.
Heavy as a statuary, shapes not ours Performed a dumbshow in the
polished wood, That cabinet without windows or doors:
He lifts an arm to bring her close, but she Shies from his touch: his
is an iron mood. Seeing her freeze, he turns his face away. They poise
and grieve as in some old tragedy.
Moon-blanched and implacable, he and she Would not be eased,
released. Our each example Of temderness dove through their
purgatory
Like a planet, a stone, swallowed in a great darkness, Leaving no
sparky track, setting up no ripple.
Nightly we left them in their desert place.
Lights out, they dogged us, sleepless and envious:
We dreamed their arguments, their stricken voices.
We might embrace, but those two never did,
Come, so unlike us, to a stiff impasse,
Burdened in such a way we seemed the lighter-
Ourselves the haunters, and they, flesh and blood;
As if, above love's ruinage, we were
The heaven those two dreamed of, in despair.

The Queen's Complaint

In ruck and quibble of courtfolk
This giant hulked, I tell you, on her scene With hands like derricks,
Looks fierce and black as rooks;
Why, all the windows broke when he stalked in.
Her dainty acres he ramped through
And used her gentle doves with manners rude; I do not know
What fury urged him slay
Her antelope who meant him naught but good.
She spoke most chiding in his ear
Till he some pity took upon her crying; Of rich attire
He made her shoulders bare
And solaced her, but quit her at cock's crowing.
A hundred heralds she sent out
To summon in her slight all doughty men Whose force might fit
Shape of her sleep, her thought-
None of that greenhorn lot matched her bright crown.
So she is come to this rare pass
Whereby she treks in blood through sun and squall
And sings you thus :
'How sad, alas, it is
To see my people shrunk so small, so small.'

The Rival

If the moon smiled, she would resemble you. You leave the same
impression
Of something beautiful, but annihilating. Both of you are great light
borrowers.
Her O-mouth grieves at the world; yours is unaffected,
And your first gift is making stone out of everything. I wake to a
mausoleum; you are here,
Ticking your fingers on the marble table, looking for cigarettes,
Spiteful as a woman, but not so nervous,
And dying to say something unanswerable.
The moon, too, abuses her subjects, But in the daytime she is
ridiculous. Your dissatisfactions, on the other hand,
Arrive through the mailslot with loving regularity, White and blank,
expansive as carbon monoxide.
No day is safe from news of you,
Walking about in Africa maybe, but thinking of me.

The Sleepers

No map traces the street Where those two sleepers are.
We have lost track of it.
They lie as if under water In a blue, unchanging light,
The French window ajar
Curtained with yellow lace. Through the narrow crack
Odors of wet earth rise.
The snail leaves a silver track; Dark thickets hedge the house.
We take a backward look.
Among petals pale as death And leaves steadfast in shape
They sleep on, mouth to mouth. A white mist is going up.
The small green nostrils breathe, And they turn in their sleep.
Ousted from that warm bed We are a dream they dream.
Their eyelids keep up the shade. No harm can come to them.
We cast our skins and slide Into another time.

The Swarm

Somebody is shooting at something in our town --
A dull pom, pom in the Sunday street.
Jealousy can open the blood, It can make black roses.
Who are the shooting at?
It is you the knives are out for
At Waterloo, Waterloo, Napoleon,
The hump of Elba on your short back,
And the snow, marshaling its brilliant cutlery
Mass after mass, saying Shh!
Shh! These are chess people you play with, Still figures of ivory.
The mud squirms with throats, Stepping stones for French bootsoles.
The gilt and pink domes of Russia melt and float off
In the furnace of greed. Clouds, clouds. So the swarm balls and
deserts Seventy feet up, in a black pine tree.
It must be shot down. Pom! Pom!
So dumb it thinks bullets are thunder.
It thinks they are the voice of God
Condoning the beak, the claw, the grin of the dog
Yellow-haunched, a pack-dog,
Grinning over its bone of ivory
Like the pack, the pack, like everybody.
The bees have got so far. Seventy feet high! Russia, Poland and
Germany!
The mild hills, the same old magenta Fields shrunk to a penny
Spun into a river, the river crossed.
The bees argue, in their black ball,
A flying hedgehog, all prickles.
The man with gray hands stands under the honeycomb
Of their dream, the hived station
Where trains, faithful to their steel arcs,
Leave and arrive, and there is no end to the country.
Pom! Pom! They fall

Dismembered, to a tod of ivy.
So much for the charioteers, the outriders, the Grand Army!
A red tatter, Napoleon!
The last badge of victory.
The swarm is knocked into a cocked straw hat. Elba,
Elba, bleb on the sea!
The white busts of marshals, admirals, generals

Worming themselves into niches. How instructive this is!
The dumb, banded bodies
Walking the plank draped with Mother France's upholstery Into a
new mausoleum,
An ivory palace, a crotch pine.
The man with gray hands smiles --
The smile of a man of business, intensely practical.
They are not hands at all
But asbestos receptacles.
Pom! Pom! 'They would have killed me.'
Stings big as drawing pins!
It seems bees have a notion of honor, A black intractable mind.
Napoleon is pleased, he is pleased with everything.
O Europe! O ton of honey!

The Thin People

They are always with us, the thin people
Meager of dimension as the gray people
On a movie-screen. They Are unreal, we say:
It was only in a movie, it was only
In a war making evil headlines when we
Were small that they famished and Grew so lean and would not round
Out their stalky limbs again though peace
Plumped the bellies of the mice
Under the meanest table.
It was during the long hunger-battle
They found their talent to persevere In thinness, to come, later,
Into our bad dreams, their menace Not guns, not abuses,
But a thin silence.
Wrapped in flea-ridded donkey skins,
Empty of complaint, forever
Drinking vinegar from tin cups: they wore
The insufferable nimbus of the lot-drawn Scapegoat.
But so thin,
So weedy a race could not remain in dreams,
Could not remain outlandish victims
In the contracted country of the head
Any more than the old woman in her mud hut could
Keep from cutting fat meat
Out of the side of the generous moon when it
Set foot nightly in her yard Until her knife had pared
The moon to a rind of little light.
Now the thin people do not obliterate
Themselves as the dawn
Grayness blues, reddens, and the outline
Of the world comes clear and fills with color.

They persist in the sunlit room: the wallpaper

Frieze of cabbage-roses and cornflowers pales
Under their thin-lipped smiles,
Their withering kingship.
How they prop each other up!
We own no wilderness rich and deep enough
For stronghold against their stiff
Battalions. See, how the tree boles flatten
And lose their good browns
If the thin people simply stand in the forest,
Making the world go thin as a wasp's nest
And grayer; not even moving their bones.

Three Women

A Poem for Three Voices
Setting: A Maternity Ward and round about
FIRST VOICE:
I am slow as the world. I am very patient,
Turning through my time, the suns and stars
Regarding me with attention.
The moon's concern is more personal:
She passes and repasses, luminous as a nurse.
Is she sorry for what will happen? I do not think so.
She is simply astonished at fertility.
When I walk out, I am a great event.
I do not have to think, or even rehearse.
What happens in me will happen without attention.
The pheasant stands on the hill;
He is arranging his brown feathers.
I cannot help smiling at what it is I know.
Leaves and petals attend me. I am ready.
SECOND VOICE:
When I first saw it, the small red seep,
I did not believe it.
I watched the men walk about me in the office.
They were so flat!
There was something about them like cardboard, and now
I had caught it, That flat, flat, flatness from which ideas, destructions,
Bulldozers, guillotines, white chambers of shrieks proceed, Endlessly
proceed--and the cold angels, the abstractions.
I sat at my desk in my stockings, my high heels,
And the man I work for laughed:
'Have you seen something awful?
You are so white, suddenly.' And I said nothing.
I saw death in the bare trees, a deprivation.
I could not believe it. Is it so difficult
For the spirit to conceive a face, a mouth?

The letters proceed from these black keys,
and these black keys proceed
From my alphabetical fingers, ordering parts,
Parts, bits, cogs, the shining multiples.
I am dying as I sit. I lose a dimension.
Trains roar in my ears, departures, departures! The silver track of
time empties into the distance, The white sky empties of its promise,
like a cup. These are my feet, these mechanical echoes.
Tap, tap, tap, steel pegs. I am found wanting.
This is a disease I carry home, this is a death.
Again, this is a death. Is it the air,
The particles of destruction I suck up? Am I a pulse That wanes and
wanes, facing the cold angel?
Is this my lover then? This death, this death? As a child I loved a
lichen-bitten name.

Is this the one sin then, this old dead love of death?
THIRD VOICE:
I remember the minute when I knew for sure.
The willows were chilling,
The face in the pool was beautiful, but not mine-- It had a
consequential look, like everything else, And all I could see was
dangers: doves and words,
Stars and showers of gold--conceptions, conceptions!
I remember a white, cold wing
And the great swan, with its terrible look,
Coming at me, like a castle, from the top of the river.
There is a snake in swans.
He glided by; his eye had a black meaning.
I saw the world in it--small, mean and black,
Every little word hooked to every little word,
and act to act.
A hot blue day had budded into something.
I wasn't ready. The white clouds rearing
Aside were dragging me in four directions.
I wasn't ready.
I had no reverence.

I thought I could deny the consequence--
But it was too late for that.
It was too late, and the face
Went on shaping itself with love, as if
I was ready.
SECOND VOICE:
It is a world of snow now.
I am not at home.
How white these sheets are.
The faces have no features.
They are bald and impossible, like the faces of my children,
Those little sick ones that elude my arms.
Other children do not touch me: they are terrible.
They have too many colors, too much life.
They are not quiet, Quiet, like the little emptinesses
I carry.
I have had my chances.
I have tried and tried.
I have stitched life into me like a rare organ,
And walked carefully, precariously, like something rare.
I have tried not to think too hard. I have tried to be natural.
I have tried to be blind in love, like other women,
Blind in my bed, with my dear blind sweet one,
Not looking, through the thick dark, for the face of another.
I did not look. But still the face was there,
The face of the unborn one that loved its perfections,
The face of the dead one that could only be perfect
In its easy peace, could only keep holy so.
And then there were other faces. The faces of nations,
Governments, parliaments, societies,
The faceless faces of important men.

It is these men I mind:
They are so jealous of anything that is not flat!
They are jealous gods
That would have the whole world flat because they are.
I see the Father conversing with the Son.

Such flatness cannot but be holy.
'Let us make a heaven,' they say.
'Let us flatten and launder the grossness
from these souls.'

FIRST VOICE:
I am calm. I am calm.
It is the calm before something awful:
The yellow minute before the wind walks, when the leaves
Turn up their hands, their pallors. It is so quiet here.
The sheets, the faces, are white and stopped, like clocks.
Voices stand back and flatten.
Their visible hieroglyphs
Flatten to parchment screens to keep the wind off.
They paint such secrets in Arabic, Chinese!
I am dumb and brown. I am a seed about to break.
The brownness is my dead self, and it is sullen:
It does not wish to be more, or different.
Dusk hoods me in blue now, like a Mary.
O color of distance and forgetfulness!--
When will it be, the second when
Time breaks And eternity engulfs it, and I drown utterly?
I talk to myself, myself only, set apart--
Swabbed and lurid with disinfectants, sacrificial.
Waiting lies heavy on my lids. It lies like sleep,
Like a big sea. Far off, far off,
I feel the first wave tug
Its cargo of agony toward me, inescapable, tidal.
And I, a shell, echoing on this white beach
Face the voices that overwhelm, the terrible element.
THIRD VOICE:
I am a mountain now, among mountainy women.
The doctors move among us as if our bigness
Frightened the mind.
They smile like fools.
They are to blame for what I am, and they know it.
They hug their flatness like a kind of health.

And what if they found themselves surprised, as I did?
They would go mad with it.
And what if two lives leaked between my thighs?
I have seen the white clean chamber
with its instruments.
It is a place of shrieks. It is not happy.
'This is where you will come when you are ready.'
The night lights are flat red moons.
They are dull with blood.
I am not ready for anything to happen.
I should have murdered this, that murders me.
FIRST VOICE:
There is no miracle more cruel than this.

I am dragged by the horses, the iron hooves.
I last. I last it out. I accomplish a work.
Dark tunnel, through which hurtle the visitations,
The visitations, the manifestations, the startled faces.
I am the center of an atrocity.
What pains, what sorrows must I be mothering?
Can such innocence kill and kill? It milks my life.
The trees wither in the street.
The rain is corrosive.
I taste it on my tongue, and the workable horrors,
The horrors that stand and idle, the slighted godmothers
With their hearts that tick and tick, with their satchels of instruments.
I shall be a wall and a roof, protecting.
I shall be a sky and a hill of good: O let me be!
A power is growing on me, an old tenacity.
I am breaking apart like the world. There is this blackness,
This ram of blackness. I fold my hands on a mountain.
The air is thick. It is thick with this working. I am used.
I am drummed into use.
My eyes are squeezed by this blackness.
I see nothing.
SECOND VOICE:
I am accused. I dream of massacres.

I am a garden of black and red agonies.
I drink them,
Hating myself, hating and fearing.
And now the world conceives
Its end and runs toward it, arms held out in love.
It is a love of death that sickens everything.
A dead sun stains the newsprint. It is red.
I lose life after life.
The dark earth drinks them.
She is the vampire of us all.
So she supports us, Fattens us, is kind.
Her mouth is red.
I know her.
I know her intimately--
Old winter-face, old barren one, old time bomb.
Men have used her meanly. She will eat them.
Eat them, eat them, eat them in the end.
The sun is down. I die. I make a death.
FIRST VOICE:
Who is he, this blue, furious boy,
Shiny and strange, as if he had hurtled from a star?
He is looking so angrily!
He flew into the room, a shriek at his heel.
The blue color pales. He is human after all.
A red lotus opens in its bowl of blood;
They are stitching me up with silk, as if
I were a material.
What did my fingers do before they held him?
What did my heart do, with its love?
I have never seen a thing so clear.

His lids are like the lilac-flower
And soft as a moth, his breath.
I shall not let go.
There is no guile or warp in him.
May he keep so.
SECOND VOICE:

There is the moon in the high window. It is over.
How winter fills my soul! And that chalk light
Laying its scales on the windows, the windows of empty offices,
Empty schoolrooms, empty churches. O so much emptiness!
There is this cessation. This terrible cessation of everything.
These bodies mounded around me now, these polar sleepers--
What blue, moony ray ices their dreams?
I feel it enter me, cold, alien, like an instrument.
And that mad, hard face at the end of it, that
O-mouth Open in its gape of perpetual grieving.
It is she that drags the blood-black sea around
Month after month, with its voices of failure.
I am helpless as the sea at the end of her string.
I am restless. Restless and useless. I, too, create corpses.
I shall move north. I shall move into a long blackness. I see myself
as a shadow, neither man nor woman, Neither a woman, happy to be
like a man, nor a man Blunt and flat enough to feel no lack.
I feel a lack.
I hold my fingers up, ten white pickets.
See, the darkness is leaking from the cracks.
I cannot contain it. I cannot contain my life.
I shall be a heroine of the peripheral.
I shall not be accused by isolate buttons,
Holes in the heels of socks, the white mute faces Of unanswered
letters, coffined in a letter case.
I shall not be accused, I shall not be accused.
The clock shall not find me wanting, nor these stars
That rivet in place abyss after abyss.
THIRD VOICE:
I see her in my sleep, my red, terrible girl.
She is crying through the glass that separates us.
She is crying, and she is furious.
Her cries are hooks that catch and grate like cats.
It is by these hooks she climbs to my notice.
She is crying at the dark, or at the stars
That at such a distance from us shine and whirl.
I think her little head is carved in wood,

A red, hard wood, eyes shut and mouth wide open. And from the
open mouth issue sharp cries Scratching at my sleep like arrows,
Scratching at my sleep, and entering my side.
My daughter has no teeth. Her mouth is wide. It utters such dark
sounds it cannot be good.
FIRST VOICE:
What is it that flings these innocent souls at us? Look, they are so
exhausted, they are all flat out
In their canvas-sided cots, names tied to their wrists, The little silver
trophies they've come so far for.
There are some with thick black hair, there are some bald. Their skin
tints are pink or sallow, brown or red;
They are beginning to remember their differences.
I think they are made of water; they have no expression. Their
features are sleeping, like light on quiet water.
They are the real monks and nuns in their identical garments. I see
them showering like stars on to the world--
On India, Africa, America, these miraculous ones, These pure, small
images. They smell of milk.
Their footsoles are untouched. They are walkers of air.
Can nothingness be so prodigal? Here is my son.
His wide eye is that general, flat blue.
He is turning to me like a little, blind, bright plant. One cry. It is the
hook I hang on.
And I am a river of milk. I am a warm hill.
SECOND VOICE:
I am not ugly. I am even beautiful.
The mirror gives back a woman without deformity.
The nurses give back my clothes, and an identity.
It is usual, they say, for such a thing to happen.
It is usual in my life, and the lives of others.
I am one in five, something like that.
I am not hopeless. I am beautiful as a statistic.
Here is my lipstick.
I draw on the old mouth.
The red mouth I put by with my identity
A day ago, two days, three days ago.

It was a Friday. I do not even need a holiday;
I can go to work today. I can love my husband,
who will understand.
Who will love me through the blur of my deformity
As if I had lost an eye, a leg, a tongue.
And so I stand, a little sightless. So I walk
Away on wheels, instead of legs, they serve as well. And learn to
speak with fingers, not a tongue.
The body is resourceful.
The body of a starfish can grow back its arms And newts are
prodigal in legs. And may I be As prodigal in what lacks me.

THIRD VOICE:
She is a small island, asleep and peaceful,
And I am a white ship hooting: Goodbye, goodbye.
The day is blazing. It is very mournful.
The flowers in this room are red and tropical.
They have lived behind glass all their lives, they have been cared for
tenderly.
Now they face a winter of white sheets, white faces.
There is very little to go into my suitcase.
There are the clothes of a fat woman
I do not know. There is my comb and brush.
There is an emptiness. I am so vulnerable suddenly.
I am a wound walking out of hospital.
I am a wound that they are letting go.
I leave my health behind. I leave someone
Who would adhere to me: I undo her fingers like bandages:
I go.
SECOND VOICE:
I am myself again. There are no loose ends.
I am bled white as wax, I have no attachments.
I am flat and virginal, which means nothing
 has happened,
Nothing that cannot be erased, ripped up and scrapped,
 begun again. There little black twigs do not think to bud,
Nor do these dry, dry gutters dream of rain.

This woman who meets me in windows--she is neat.
So neat she is transparent, like a spirit. how shyly she superimposes
                                                her neat self
On the inferno of African oranges, the heel-hung pigs.
                                She is deferring to reality.
                                        It is I. It is I--
Tasting the bitterness between my teeth.
The incalculable malice of the everyday.
                                        FIRST VOICE:
How long can I be a wall, keeping the wind off? How long can I be
Gentling the sun with the shade of my hand, Intercepting the blue
bolts of a cold moon? The voices of loneliness, the voices of sorrow
                                Lap at my back ineluctably.
                        How shall it soften them, this little lullaby?
                How long can I be a wall around my green property?
                                        How long can my hands
                        Be a bandage to his hurt, and my words
                Bright birds in the sky, consoling, consoling?
                                        It is a terrible thing
                                To be so open: it is as if my heart
                        Put on a face and walked into the world.

                                        THIRD VOICE:
                        Today the colleges are drunk with spring.
                                My black gown is a little funeral:
                                        It shows I am serious.
                        The books I carry wedge into my side.
I had an old wound once, but it is healing. I had a dream of an island,
                red with cries. It was a dream, and did not mean a thing.
                                        FIRST VOICE:
                Dawn flowers in the great elm outside the house.
                                        The swifts are back.
                        They are shrieking like paper rockets.
                                I hear the sound of the hours
                                Widen and die in the hedgerows.
                                        I hear the moo of cows.
                The colors replenish themselves, and the wet

Thatch smokes in the sun.
The narcissi open white faces in the orchard.
I am reassured. I am reassured.
These are the clear bright colors of the nursery,
The talking ducks, the happy lambs.
I am simple again. I believe in miracles.
I do not believe in those terrible children
Who injure my sleep with their white eyes, their fingerless hands.
They are not mine. They do not belong to me.
I shall meditate upon normality.
I shall meditate upon my little son.
He does not walk. He does not speak a word.
He is still swaddled in white bands.
But he is pink and perfect. He smiles so frequently.
I have papered his room with big roses,
I have painted little hearts on everything.
I do not will him to be exceptional.
It is the exception that interests the devil.
It is the exception that climbs the sorrowful hill
Or sits in the desert and hurts his mother's heart.
I will him to be common,
To love me as I love him,
And to marry what he wants and where he will.
THIRD VOICE:
Hot noon in the meadows.
The buttercups Swelter and melt, and the lovers
Pass by, pass by.
They are black and flat as shadows.
It is so beautiful to have no attachments!
I am solitary as grass. What is it I miss?
Shall I ever find it, whatever it is?

The swans are gone. Still the river
Remembers how white they were.
It strives after them with its lights.
It finds their shapes in a cloud.
What is that bird that cries

With such sorrow in its voice?
I am young as ever, it says. What is it I miss?
SECOND VOICE:
I am at home in the lamplight. The evenings are lengthening. I am
mending a silk slip: my husband is reading.
How beautifully the light includes these things.
There is a kind of smoke in the spring air,
A smoke that takes the parks, the little statues
With pinkness, as if a tenderness awoke,
A tenderness that did not tire, something healing.
I wait and ache. I think I have been healing.
There is a great deal else to do. My hands
Can stitch lace neatly on to this material.
My husband Can turn and turn the pages of a book.
And so we are at home together, after hours.
It is only time that weighs upon our hands.
It is only time, and that is not material.
The streets may turn to paper suddenly, but
I recover From the long fall, and find myself in bed,
Safe on the mattress, hands braced, as for a fall.
I find myself again. I am no shadow
Though there is a shadow starting from my feet. I am a wife.
The city waits and aches.
The little grasses
Crack through stone, and they are green with life.

Totem

The engine is killing the track, the track is silver,
It stretches into the distance. It will be eaten nevertheless.
Its running is useless.
At nightfall there is the beauty of drowned fields,
Dawn gilds the farmers like pigs, Swaying slightly in their thick suits,
White towers of Smithfield ahead,
Fat haunches and blood on their minds.
There is no mercy in the glitter of cleavers,
The butcher's guillotine that whispers: 'How's this, how's this?'
In the bowl the hare is aborted,
Its baby head out of the way, embalmed in spice,
Flayed of fur and humanity.
Let us eat it like Plato's afterbirth,
Let us eat it like Christ.
These are the people that were important ----
Their round eyes, their teeth, their grimaces
On a stick that rattles and clicks, a counterfeit snake.
Shall the hood of the cobra appall me ----
The loneliness of its eye, the eye of the mountains
Through which the sky eternally threads itself?
The world is blood-hot and personal
Dawn says, with its blood-flush.
There is no terminus, only suitcases
Out of which the same self unfolds like a suit
Bald and shiny, with pockets of wishes,
Notions and tickets, short circuits and folding mirrors.
I am mad, calls the spider, waving its many arms.
And in truth it is terrible,
Multiplied in the eyes of the flies.
They buzz like blue children In nets of the infinite,
Roped in at the end by the one
Death with its many sticks.

Tulips

The tulips are too excitable, it is winter here.
Look how white everything is, how quiet, how snowed-in I am
learning peacefulness, lying by myself quietly
As the light lies on these white walls, this bed, these hands. I am
nobody; I have nothing to do with explosions.
I have given my name and my day-clothes up to the nurses And my
history to the anaesthetist and my body to surgeons.
They have propped my head between the pillow and the sheet-cuff
Like an eye between two white lids that will not shut.
Stupid pupil, it has to take everything in.
The nurses pass and pass, they are no trouble,
They pass the way gulls pass inland in their white caps, Doing things
with their hands, one just the same as another, So it is impossible to
tell how many there are.
My body is a pebble to them, they tend it as water
Tends to the pebbles it must run over, smoothing them gently.
They bring me numbness in their bright needles, they bring me sleep.
Now I have lost myself I am sick of baggage ----
My patent leather overnight case like a black pillbox, My husband and
child smiling out of the family photo; Their smiles catch onto my
skin, little smiling hooks.
I have let things slip, a thirty-year-old cargo boat Stubbornly hanging
on to my name and address.
They have swabbed me clear of my loving associations.
Scared and bare on the green plastic-pillowed trolley
I watched my teaset, my bureaus of linen,
my books Sink out of sight, and
the water went over my head.
I am a nun now, I have never been so pure.
I didn't want any flowers,
I only wanted
To lie with my hands turned up and be utterly empty.

How free it is, you have no idea how free ----
The peacefulness is so big it dazes you,
And it asks nothing, a name tag, a few trinkets.
It is what the dead close on, finally;
I imagine them Shutting their mouths on it, like a
Communion tablet.
The tulips are too red in the first place, they hurt me.
Even through the gift paper
I could hear them breathe Lightly, through their white swaddlings,
like an awful baby. Their redness talks to my wound, it corresponds.
They are subtle: they seem to float, though they weigh me down,
Upsetting me with their sudden tongues and their colour,
A dozen red lead sinkers round my neck.
Nobody watched me before, now I am watched.
The tulips turn to me, and the window behind me
Where once a day the light slowly widens and slowly thins,
And I see myself, flat, ridiculous, a cut-paper shadow

Between the eye of the sun and the eyes of the tulips,
And I hve no face, I have wanted to efface myself.
The vivid tulips eat my oxygen.
Before they came the air was calm enough,
Coming and going, breath by breath, without any fuss.
Then the tulips filled it up like a loud noise.
Now the air snags and eddies round them the way a river
Snags and eddies round a sunken rust-red engine.
They concentrate my attention, that was happy
Playing and resting without committing itself.
The walls, also, seem to be warming themselves.
The tulips should be behind bars like dangerous animals;
They are opening like the mouth of some great
African cat, And I am aware of my heart: it opens
and closes
Its bowl of red blooms out of sheer love of me.
The water I taste is warm and salt, like the sea,
And comes from a country far away as health.

Two Campers in Cloud Country

(Rock Lake, Canada)
In this country there is neither measure nor balance
To redress the dominance of rocks and woods,
The passage, say, of these man-shaming clouds.
No gesture of yours or mine could catch their attention, No word
make them carry water or fire the kindling
Like local trolls in the spell of a superior being.
Well, one wearies of the Public Gardens: one wants a vacation
Where trees and clouds and animals pay no notice;
Away from the labeled elms, the tame tea-roses.
It took three days driving north to find a cloud
The polite skies over Boston couldn't possibly accommodate.
Here on the last frontier of the big, brash spirit
The horizons are too far off to be chummy as uncles;
The colors assert themselves with a sort of vengeance.
Each day concludes in a huge splurge of vermilions
And night arrives in one gigantic step.
It is comfortable, for a change, to mean so little.
These rocks offer no purchase to herbage or people:
They are conceiving a dynasty of perfect cold.
In a month we'll wonder what plates and forks are for. I lean to you,
numb as a fossil. Tell me I'm here.
The Pilgrims and Indians might never have happened.
Planets pulse in the lake like bright amoebas;
The pines blot our voices up in their lightest sighs.
Around our tent the old simplicities sough
Sleepily as Lethe, trying to get in.
We'll wake blank-brained as water in the dawn.

Two Sisters of Persephone

Two girls there are : within the house
One sits; the other, without.
Daylong a duet of shade and light
Plays between these.
In her dark wainscoted room
The first works problems on A mathematical machine.
Dry ticks mark time
As she calculates each sum.
At this barren enterprise
Rat-shrewd go her squint eyes,
Root-pale her meager frame.

Bronzed as earth, the second lies,
Hearing ticks blown gold
Like pollen on bright air. Lulled
Near a bed of poppies,
She sees how their red silk flare
Of petaled blood
Burns open to the sun's blade.
On that green alter
Freely become sun's bride, the latter
Grows quick with seed.
Grass-couched in her labor's pride,
She bears a king. Turned bitter
And sallow as any lemon,
The other, wry virgin to the last,
Goes graveward with flesh laid waste,
Worm-husbanded, yet no woman.

Two Views of a Cadaver Room

1

The day she visited the dissecting room
They had four men laid out, black as burnt turkey, Already half
unstrung. A vinegary fume
Of the death vats clung to them;
The white-smocked boys started working. The head of his cadaver
had caved in, And she could scarcely make out anything
In that rubble of skull plates and old leather. A sallow piece of string
held it together.
In their jars the snail-nosed babies moon and glow.
He hands her the cut-out heart like a cracked heirloom.

2

In Brueghel's panorama of smoke and slaughter Two people only are
blind to the carrion army: He, afloat in the sea of her blue satin
Skirts, sings in the direction
Of her bare shoulder, while she bends, Finger a leaflet of music, over
him,
Both of them deaf to the fiddle in the hands Of the death's-head
shadowing their song. These Flemish lovers flourish;not for long.
Yet desolation, stalled in paint, spares the little country Foolish,
delicate, in the lower right hand corner

Vanity Fair

Through frost-thick weather
This witch sidles, fingers crooked, as if
Caught in a hazardous medium that might
Merely by its continuing
Attach her to heaven.
At eye's envious corner
Crow's-feet copy veining on a stained leaf;
Cold squint steals sky's color; while bruit
Of bells calls holy ones, her tongue
Backtalks at the raven
Claeving furred air
Over her skull's midden; no knife
Rivals her whetted look, divining what conceit
Waylays simple girls, church-going,
And what heart's oven
Craves most to cook batter
Rich in strayings with every amorous oaf,
Ready, for a trinket,
To squander owl-hours on bracken bedding,
Flesh unshriven.
Against virgin prayer
This sorceress sets mirrors enough
To distract beauty's thought; Lovesick at first fond song,
Each vain girl's driven
To believe beyond heart's flare No fire is, nor in any book proof
Sun hoists soul up after lids fall shut;
So she wills all to the black king.
The worst sloven
Vies with best queen over Right to blaze as satan's wife;
Housed in earth, those million brides shriek out.
Some burn short, some long,
Staked in pride's coven.
Anonymous submission.

Virgin in a Tree

How this tart fable instructs
And mocks! Here's the parody of that moral mousetrap Set in the
proverbs stitched on samplers
Approving chased girls who get them to a tree
And put on bark's nun-black
Habit which deflects
All amorous arrows. For to sheathe the virgin shape
In a scabbard of wood baffles pursuers,
Whether goat-thighed or god-haloed. Ever since that first Daphne
Switched her incomparable back
For a bay-tree hide, respect's
Twined to her hard limbs like ivy: the puritan lip Cries: '
Celebrate Syrinx whose demurs
Won her the frog-colored skin, pale pith and watery
Bed of a reed. Look:
Pine-needle armor protects
Pitys from Pan's assault! And though age drop
Their leafy crowns, their fame soars,
Eclipsing Eva, Cleo and Helen of Troy:
For which of those would speak
For a fashion that constricts
White bodies in a wooden girdle, root to top Unfaced, unformed, the
nipple-flowers Shrouded to suckle darkness?
Only they Who keep cool and holy make
A sanctum to attract
Green virgins, consecrating limb and lip
To chastity's service: like prophets, like preachers,
They descant on the serene and seraphic beauty
Of virgins for virginity's sake.'
Be certain some such pact's
Been struck to keep all glory in the grip
Of ugly spinsters and barren sirs
As you etch on the inner window of your eye

This virgin on her rack:
She, ripe and unplucked, 's
Lain splayed too long in the tortuous boughs: overripe
Now, dour-faced, her fingers
Stiff as twigs, her body woodenly
Askew, she'll ache and wake
Though doomsday bud. Neglect's
Given her lips that lemon-tasting droop:
Untongued, all beauty's bright juice sours.
Tree-twist will ape this gross anatomy

Till irony's bough break.

Winter landscape, with rocks

Water in the millrace, through a sluice of
stone, plunges headlong into that black pond
where, absurd and out-of-season, a single swan floats chaste as snow,
taunting the clouded mind which hungers
to haul the white reflection down.
The austere sun descends above the fen, an orange cyclops-eye,
scorning to look longer on this landscape of chagrin;
feathered dark in thought, I stalk like a rook, brooding as the winter
night comes on.
Last summer's reeds are all engraved in ice as is your image in my eye;
dry frost glazes the window of my hurt; what solace
can be struck from rock to make heart's waste grow green again?
Who'd walk in this bleak place?

Winter Landscape, With Rooks

Water in the millrace, through a sluice of stone,
plunges headlong into that black pond
where, absurd and out-of-season, a single swan floats chaste as snow,
taunting the clouded mind which hungers to haul the white reflection
down.
The austere sun descends above the fen, an orange cyclops-eye,
scorning to look longer on this landscape of chagrin;
feathered dark in thought, I stalk like a rook, brooding as the winter
night comes on.
Last summer's reeds are all engraved in ice as is your image in my eye;
dry frost glazes the window of my hurt; what solace
can be struck from rock to make heart's waste grow green again?
Who'd walk in this bleak place?

Winter Trees

The wet dawn inks are doing their blue dissolve.
On their blotter of fog the trees
Seem a botanical drawing. Memories growing, ring on ring,
A series of weddings.
Knowing neither abortions nor bitchery,
Truer than women,
They seed so effortlessly!
Tasting the winds, that are footless, Waist-deep in history.
Full of wings, otherworldliness. In this, they are Ledas.
O mother of leaves and sweetness Who are these pietas?
The shadows of ringdoves chanting, but chasing nothing.